THE WORLD'S CLASSICS

EROTIC POEMS

JOHANN WOLFGANG VON GOETHE was born in 1749, the son of a well-to-do citizen of Frankfurt. As a young man he studied law and briefly practised as a lawyer, but creative writing was his chief concern. In the early 1770s he was the dominating figure of the German literary revival, his tragic novel *Werther* bringing him international fame.

In 1775 he settled permanently in the small duchy of Weimar where he became a minister of state and director of the court theatre; in 1782 he was ennobled as 'von Goethe'. His journey to Italy in 1786–8 influenced the development of his mature classical style; in the 1790s, he and his younger contemporary Schiller (1759–1805) were the joint architects of Weimar Classicism, the central phase of German literary culture.

Goethe wrote in all the literary genres but his interests extended far beyond literature and included a number of scientific subjects. *Faust*, written at various stages of his life and in a variety of styles, became a constantly enlarged repository of his personal wisdom. His creative energies never ceased to take new forms and he was still writing original poetry at the age of more than 80. In 1806 he married Christiane Vulpius (1765–1816), having lived with her for eighteen years; they had one surviving son, August (1789–1830). Goethe died in 1832.

DAVID LUKE was a Student (Fellow) and Tutor in German at Christ Church, Oxford, until 1988. He has edited and translated the Penguin Poets *Goethe* (1964) and the Oxford World's Classics *Faust Part One* (1987, awarded the European Poetry Translation Prize in 1989) and *Part Two* (1994), as well as various other works of German literature including Heinrich von Kleist's stories, the tales of the Brothers Grimm, and *Death in Venice and Other Stories* by Thomas Mann.

HANS RUDOLF VAGET is the Helen and Laura Shedd Professor of German Studies and Comparative Literature at Smith College (Northampton, Mass.). He has published extensively on Goethe, Wagner, Thomas Mann, and other subjects. In 1994 he was awarded the Thomas Mann Medal for his edition of the correspondence of Thomas Mann and Agnes E. Meyer (Frankfurt am Main, 1992).

THE WORLD'S CLASSICS

JOHANN WOLFGANG VON GOETHE

Erotic Poems

Verse translation by
DAVID LUKE

Introduction by
HANS RUDOLF VAGET

Oxford   New York
OXFORD UNIVERSITY PRESS
1997

Oxford University Press, Great Clarendon Street, Oxford OX2 6DP

Oxford New York

Athens Auckland Bangkok Bogota Bombay Buenos Aires
Calcutta Cape Town Dar es Salaam Delhi Florence. Hong Kong
Istanbul Karachi Kuala Lumpur Madras Madrid Melbourne
Mexico City Nairobi Paris Singapore Taipei Tokyo Toronto

and associated companies in
Berlin Ibadan

Oxford is a trade mark of Oxford University Press

Roman Elegies and The Diary first published in this translation in a
bilingual edition, with introduction by Hans R. Vaget, by Libris Ltd., 1988

First published as a World's Classics paperback 1997

British Library Cataloguing in Publication Data

Data available

Library of Congress Cataloging in Publication Data

Goethe, Johann Wolfgang von, 1749–1832.
[Poems. English & German. Selections]
Erotic poems / Johann Wolfgang von Goethe; verse translation by
David Luke; introduction by Hans Rudolf Vaget.
(The world's classics)
English and German.
Rev. edn. of: Roman elegies and The diary. 1988.
Includes bibliographical references and index.
Contents: Römische Elegien = Roman elegies—Aus den
Venezianischen Epigrammen = From the Venetian epigrams—Das
Tagebuch = The diary.
1. Erotic poetry, German. I. Goethe, Johann Wolfgang von, 1749–1832. Römische Elegien.
English & German. II. Luke, David, 1921– . III. Title. IV. Series.
PT2026.R6L8513 1997   831'.6—dc20   96-31080

ISBN 0-19-283270-0

1 3 5 7 9 10 8 6 4 2

Typeset by Best-set Typesetter Ltd., Hong Kong
Printed in Great Britain by
BPC Paperbacks Ltd.
Aylesbury, Bucks.

CONTENTS

PREFACE

The present bilingual edition of Goethe's erotic poetry is based on our previous publication under the title *Roman Elegies and The Diary* (Libris Books, 1988). This has been slightly revised, and in keeping with the new title an appropriate selection from the *Venetian Epigrams* has now been added.

The *Roman Elegies* have usually been printed as a cycle of twenty poems, a further four being excluded for reasons which we discuss in the Introduction. Even the massive historical–critical 'Weimarer Ausgabe' (WA)[1] prudishly relegated these to a late supplementary volume published in 1914 (liii. 3–7). We are here including the complete cycle of twenty-four, restoring the missing four elegies to their proper places in accordance with what appears to have been Goethe's original intention, and consequentially renumbering the cycle. The restored poems are now I, III, XVII, and XXIV; numbers I and XXIV have the character of a prologue and an epilogue, as we have indicated. For the actual words and punctuation of these twenty-four elegies, we have again conformed (with one important exception in Elegy XV, which we discuss in the Explanatory Notes) to Emil Staiger's Manesse Verlag edition (1949), which is complete in that it includes all twenty-four poems (even if not in the order we here propose), modern in that it uses modern spelling, and traditional in that its text for the main core of twenty elegies ultimately derives from the revised version published by Goethe in 1800 in his *Neue Schriften* (N). This revision became the basis for all subsequent canonical editions, notably Goethe's own 'final edition' (the *Ausgabe letzter Hand*) of 1827 and the WA, both of which Staiger also uses. Today we have, as well, the authoritative new forty-volume Deutscher Klassiker Verlag edition of Goethe's total output, which virtually replaces the WA; in vols. i and ii of this (1987–8) the complete poems are scrupulously presented on historical principles by Karl Eibl. In the case of the *Roman Elegies*, Eibl prints parallel texts of Goethe's original MS version and of the

---

[1] Details of the German editions here referred to are given in the Select Bibliography (1).

version first published by Schiller in his periodical *Die Horen* (the '*Horenfassung*'). For the non-specialist, however, the effect of this is confusing, and we saw no advantage in adopting either of these early and in any case defective variants in preference to the standard and now traditional 1800 text as represented by Staiger, though we have throughout referred to Eibl for comparison.

With the *Venetian Epigrams*, which Goethe regarded as a closely related work, the position is similar: modern editions must restore the fifty or sixty suppressed epigrams, adding them somehow to the traditionally accepted corpus of about a hundred. The first version of the latter appeared in December 1795 in Schiller's other periodical, an annual literary 'almanach' (*Musenalmanach für das Jahr 1796*); like the *Elegies* they were then revised by Goethe for the canonical collected editions. Many other epigrams, however, like the four offending elegies, were for over a century simply suppressed as too indecent or irreligious to print. This remaining MS material was eventually released by the Weimar Goethe archive and inconspicuously published with the missing four elegies in 1914 (WA liii. 8–18). Both Staiger and Eibl print all the epigrams, canonical and posthumous, though for the former Eibl uses the earlier *Musenalmanachfassung*. Our selection is based on Staiger's text, very occasionally substituting a reading from Eibl where this seemed preferable.

As the Introduction explains, *Das Tagebuch* was also persistently suppressed or editorially mutilated until quite recently, and there are textual problems in it which even the most modern editions do not quite resolve. We here use, with two minor corrections, the version established by Hans Rudolf Vaget in his study *Goethe: Der Mann von 60 Jahren* (1982). The translations here printed of the *Römische Elegien* and of *Das Tagebuch* correspond, with a few revisions, to the Libris edition, and in the case of Elegies II–XXIII to the version previously published by Chatto & Windus (*Roman Elegies*, 1977). As before, the Introduction is essentially the work of Hans Rudolf Vaget, with a few passages added in collaboration with David Luke. The material following the texts (Translator's Postscript and Explanatory Notes) is by David Luke, in consultation with Hans Rudolf Vaget.

D.L.

H.R.V.

INTRODUCTION

The Poet as Liberator: Goethe's Priapean Project

In a brief statement addressed, at the very end of his life, to the young poets of 1830, Goethe described himself as their 'liberator'.[1] There is abundant evidence to justify this proud self-characterization by the octogenarian poet, and some of the most striking is to be found in his erotic poetry. At virtually every stage of his career, even when he seems to be engaged in purely restorative projects such as Weimar Classicism, Goethe's poetry was breaking new ground. Although he later repudiated, and in *Faust* ironized, the gospel of original genius, Goethe as poet remained committed to innovation. This is especially true of those instances in which, seeming merely to pay tribute to tradition, he engaged with the canonical models of antiquity and transformed them, as he did in the *Roman Elegies*.

At the time when Goethe first made his mark on German and European literature, in the early 1770s, the ideal of originality, with its far-reaching implications, was asserting itself as the most seductive and powerful of the new currents of aesthetic thought that had entered the German-speaking countries from France and especially from England. Goethe's writings of his early Strasbourg and Frankfurt period, culminating in the tragic lyrical novel *The Sorrows of Young Werther* (1774), gave validity to the battle-cry for original genius and inspired the young generation's desire to be liberated from the norms of literary and social authority. Thus it was only natural that the group of 'Sturm und Drang' (Storm and Stress) writers, as they came to be known, looked to Goethe as their leader. Although this informal association was only a brief one, it left a more lasting imprint on his entire literary production than is generally realized.

It is a pleasure to acknowledge the many helpful suggestions I have received from friends and colleagues who were kind enough to read earlier versions of this essay: David Ball, Peter Bloom, Stanley Corngold, Andrew Ford, Ann Leone, David Luke, Judith Ryan.

[1] 'Further Advice for Young Poets', in *Essays on Art and Literature* (Suhrkamp edn. of Goethe's collected works in 12 vols., Suhrkamp Publishers, Boston, 1983–8), iii. 209.

To the casual observer, Goethe's youthful Storm and Stress period may appear a mere stepping-stone on the way to more mature tasks, or—to invoke one of his favourite images—a skin that had to be shed in the course of what he saw as the organic growth of his personality. A more careful reader, however, will soon realize that Goethe's entire poetic production remained grounded in the aesthetic sensibility of his early breakthrough period. The best word to describe that sensibility might well be 'pan-erotic'. At the vital core of his creative personality, this most protean of poets remained faithful to 'young Werther', his early and perhaps most authentic self-projection, long after he had 'outgrown' the fever and ecstasy associated with that name. Late in his life, in 'An Werther' ('To Werther'), the opening poem of the famous Marienbad triptych (1823/4) which he called 'Trilogie der Leidenschaft' ('Trilogy of Passion'), Goethe acknowledged as if with regret the subterranean continuity of that sensibility:

> Dann zog uns wieder ungewisse Bahn
> Der Leidenschaften labyrinthisch an.
>
> And then again, passion's uncertain maze
> Drew us into its labyrinthine ways.

We should not, however, attribute too much biographical truth to the lamenting voice of 'An Werther'. It appears that Goethe actually longed for the return of Werther and what he stood for. As he grew older, most clearly after the death of Schiller in 1805, Goethe engaged with increasing urgency in the project of recovering, through recollection and active remembrance, the creative energies of his youth. His autobiography, begun in 1809, represents only the most visible part of this enterprise. Goethe must have sensed that the more sophisticated and fragile poetic practices of his later years stood in need of the erotic energies that inform his early poetry. To the ageing Goethe, 'renewed puberty' ('wiederholte Pubertät'), as he called it in a telling and much-quoted phrase,[2] had become a biological as well as literary phantasm—but a phantasm of remarkable potency. It is in this context that a poem such as *The Diary*, which thematizes the creative force of remembering, acquires a significance beyond its more obvious narrative of erotic adventure.

[2] Conversation with Eckermann, 11 Mar. 1828. (See J. P. Eckermann, *Conversations with Goethe*, tr. J. Oxenford, Everyman's Library, Dent, 1930.)

From what did Goethe liberate German poetry? The brief essay in which he lays claim to the title of liberator does not tell us. He does not identify the fetters and conventions from which he had to free himself. Instead, he reminds his younger colleagues of the new freedom which poetry was now able to explore: the freedom to express the self. The young poets, he asserts, 'have through me become aware that, just as man must live from within, the artist must express his own self by revealing—no matter how he does it—only his own specific individuality'.[3] Simple and general though they may sound to us today, Goethe's parting words to his fellow poets make a basic point—a point that was crucial in the particular historical moment of his beginnings when both Goethe and German poetry were in their 'puberty': namely, that the poet's distinctive role is to express a world in his own authentic voice.

Goethe's statement of 1832 can be read not only as a piece of advice for young poets but, perhaps more productively, as a justification of his own poetic enterprise as a whole. No one before had put poetry so confidently at the service of self-expression and self-exploration. He had found himself at the threshold of an age that legitimized and encouraged the exploration of the self and gave it an entirely new sense of purpose. The Enlightenment had bequeathed to the Storm and Stress movement a new belief proclaiming the autonomy and wholeness of man. To young Goethe, the source of this message was Johann Georg Hamann, the friend and teacher of his own mentor Johann Gottfried Herder. Goethe's autobiography, written some forty years later, still testifies eloquently to the liberating effect of Hamann's insistence on wholeness.[4] For Hamann, however, the self was an emphatically sexual being, and genius was to be defined as creativity in both the spiritual and the sexual sense. With characteristic bluntness Hamann declared in his *Socratic Memorabilia* (1759) that a genius without genitals is not a genius.

Goethe, whose concept of 'Humanität' owes much to Hamann, has contributed more to our awareness of the nature and force of desire than is generally realized, and more than any other poet in German literature. His work is surprisingly knowledgeable about sexuality in all its manifestations, including androgyny,

[3] 'Further Advice', 209.
[4] *Poetry and Truth*, Suhrkamp edn., iv. 380 f.

homoeroticism, incest, narcissism, and fetishism. It is anything but an accident that Freud, a liberator on a different scale, turned to Goethe as one of his preferred case-studies, thus acknowledging him as a mythical precursor. It may well be argued, therefore, that to the extent that he relies on examples from the German literary imagination, 'Freud recognizes in Goethe the source and seed from which psychoanalysis was engendered'—with all the ambivalent dynamics that such paternity entails.[5]

Goethe's reputation as a poet of the erotic is well established. And yet, our knowledge of his erotic poetry in the precise sense rests on shaky foundations. The situation is nothing short of contradictory. On the one hand, generations of readers from the Romantics until today have admired the erotic freedom of his second novel *Wilhelm Meister's Apprenticeship*, the elaborate apotheosis of Eros in *Faust*, and the spiritualized eroticism of *The West-Eastern Divan*, which contains, arguably, the most sustained cycle of love poems in the German language. On the other hand, however, there exists as yet no complete and universal appreciation of Goethe's explicitly sexual poetry, the poems that speak of 'true, naked love'—'den echten, nackteten Amor' (Elegy III). This includes, apart from the *Roman Elegies*, a good number of his *Venetian Epigrams*, as well as his *summum opus* in this vein, *The Diary*. To be sure, the *Roman Elegies* are now generally held in high esteem; most readers today would agree with E. M. Wilkinson's assessment of the *Elegies* as a work of unique originality: 'in their plastic beauty and unabashed sensuality, their blending of erotic tenderness with an enhanced sense of our cultural heritage, these pagan, highly civilized poems are unique in any modern language'.[6] How odd then that Goethe's Roman cycle has never, until now, been presented to the general public in its entirety and its original design. Most readers know it only in a truncated form. The same is true of the *Venetian Epigrams*. And Goethe's most daring and profound erotic poem, *The Diary*, is hardly known at all.

Whatever other conclusion we may draw from this paradoxical

[5] A. Ronell, *Dictations: On Haunted Writing* (Indiana University Press, 1986).
[6] E. M. Wilkinson, article on Goethe in *The New Encyclopaedia Britannica (Macropedia)*, xx. 184. See also D. J. Enright, 'Goethe's "Roman Elegies"', *Scrutiny*, 15 (1947-8); E. M. Wilkinson, 'Sexual Attitudes in Goethe's Life and Works', in id. (ed.), *Goethe Revisited* (Calder, 1984).

situation, it offers above all a clear object-lesson in the power of literary and social convention. That power is manifest, for instance, in Goethe's own diplomatic, though reluctant, self-censorship, and (with much less justification) in the long-standing refusal of Goethe scholars to admit *The Diary* and the suppressed parts of the *Roman Elegies* and of the *Venetian Epigrams* into the canon of his works. Beyond the obvious moral and social reasons for this stubborn misrepresentation, it is doubtless, ultimately, rooted in the innovative nature of Goethe's writing about the erotic. His poems in this genre, especially *The Diary*, mark such a bold break with the conventions of the older erotic poetry of the eighteenth century that for a long time, until recently in fact, they found only a few appreciative readers. Goethe's erotic poetry transcended, in a number of different ways, what H. R. Jauss has termed the 'horizon of expectation'.[7] Most notably, it broke with a powerful convention that had governed erotic poetry for centuries. In Roman literature, erotic poetry dealt with the famous 'quinque lineae amoris', the five typical stages of erotic encounter: 'visus', 'allocutio', 'tactus', 'basium', 'coitus'—seeing, addressing, touching, kissing, and union.[8] Western love poetry since the Middle Ages and the Renaissance traditionally had to restrict itself to, at the most, four of the five classical stages. Writing explicitly of all five, as Goethe did in the *Roman Elegies* and *The Diary*, and writing about them in a serious rather than a comic vein—as had been common practice—constituted a violation of one of the strongest taboos of Western literature.

The extent to which the *Roman Elegies*, with their full-bodied celebration of sexual love, and *The Diary*, with its seemingly antithetical theme of sexual failure, are in fact linked has never been clearly recognized. What unites these two major texts as well as the thematically more varied *Venetian Epigrams* is the ambition to create a new type of erotic poetry—poems set in the contemporary world and informed by an authentically modern sensibility. For the first essay in this genre, inevitably, the great Roman models had to serve as point of departure. In post-classical, Christian Europe, the only

[7] See H. R. Jauss, *Towards an Aesthetic of Reception*, tr. T. Bahti (University of Minnesota Press, 1982), 22 f.

[8] See Karl Hehn, 'Quinque lineae amoris', *Germanisch-Romanische Monatsschrift*, 29 (1941); H. R. Vaget, 'Goethe als erotischer Dichter', in W. Wittkowski (ed.), *Verlorene Klassik?* (Niemeyer, 1986).

way for poetry to explore the vast territory beyond the boundaries of convention was by mimicking the ancients and by borrowing their gestures and inflections. Thus Goethe turned quite consciously, and self-consciously, to the famous 'triumvirate' of Catullus, Tibullus, and Propertius (cf. Elegy VII). By reviving their canonical *erotica* in his own *Erotica Romana*, as the *Elegies* were first entitled, he placed himself under the protection, as it were, of their unassailable literary authority. But donning a classicist's cloak was as much a matter of poetic strategy as it was of prudence. It endowed these modern elegies with a rich intertextual resonance and thereby lifted them beyond the reach of the kind of biographical curiosity that had plagued Goethe ever since *Werther* (cf. Elegy IV).

Two decades later he turned to an even greater challenge when he set the same kind of uninhibited, explicit, and serious *erotica* that he had realized so happily in the *Elegies* in the contemporary world of 1800—complete with business trip, hotel, erotic encounter on the road, and loving wife at home. And, more fully than in the *Elegies*, he immersed this kind of writing about sexuality in an unmistakably contemporary bourgeois sensibility that wavers uneasily between obligation and passion—'Pflicht' and 'Liebe'—the two pivotal concepts in the official legal and religious discourse on sexuality.

The new erotic poetry Goethe aimed at was to be different from the poems and verse novellas by his contemporaries Christoph Martin Wieland and Wilhelm Heinse; it was also to mark a complete break with his own early poetry written in the French rococo style of the period with its languishing and teasing and its general air of inauthenticity. Goethe's project, if we were to believe the experts, was doomed to be thwarted. Heinz Schlaffer, in his authoritative *Musa iocosa* (1971), has traced the history of erotic poetry in Germany to about 1770. The poetry written thereafter, that is, after the emergence of a distinct middle class in Germany, is dismissed as unrepresentative of middle-class morality, or as derivative of classical models. Erotic poetry, Schlaffer argues, proposes a lifestyle devoted to pleasure; it revolves around the promiscuity of independent persons without the restrictions of family ties. Accordingly, it is designated as an essentially aristocratic genre; as such it is said to be incompatible with middle-class sensibility with its emphasis on the work ethic, family, and Christian morality.[9] How does *The Diary* fit into this scheme? Astonishingly, Schlaffer simply ignores it. One can see why. Here is a major text which, according to his preconceived notions, should not exist: a modern erotic poem in a bourgeois setting, written independently of classical models and in open defiance of Christian morality.

It has long been a central tenet of neo-Marxist orthodoxy that the bourgeoisie was incapable of practising any form of truly liberated sensuality. We encounter this view even in one of the acknowledged modern masters of erotic poetry, Bertolt Brecht. Writing in his *Journals* Brecht thought it 'remarkable how we show no signs of a refined sensuality in germany'. In lyric poetry, he went on to observe, 'there is nothing between the ethereal, hysterical and incorporeal, and dirty barmaid's songs. [Gottfried] keller has certain merits. heinrich mann describes only excesses. in the middle ages this is another area of culture which only the clergy seems to have kept up. the german aristocracy was incapable of hedonism. then the bourgeoisie was puritanical in its ideals, and swinish in reality. german students "did it" after consuming beer in amounts that would have left anybody else incapable of anything but vomiting, whereas they copulated.'[10] However, Brecht did allow for two great exceptions—Goethe and Mozart. But it seems that even he was unaware of *The Diary*, and he failed to give due credit to the *Roman Elegies* on precisely the score that counted for him.

Goethe was, of course, quite conscious of the problems he faced as a modern erotic poet. In a revealing and much-quoted conversation of 25 February 1824 with his secretarial protégé Johann Peter Eckermann, he commented on some of them. He had given Eckermann two unpublished poems to read, one of which was *The Diary*. It must have been Goethe's intention on that obviously premeditated occasion to make some general observations—for the record, so to speak—on the power of convention and the detrimental influence it exerted on poetry. Eckermann played the part prescribed to him to the letter: he assured the poet that *The Diary*, at heart, was a perfectly moral work. He had to acknowledge, however,

[9] H. Schlaffer, *Musa iocosa* (Metzler, 1971), 159 f.
[10] B. Brecht, *Journals*, tr. H. Rorrison (Methuen, 1993), 8 Mar. 1941.

that the public could not but regard it as immoral on account of its 'naturalism' and forthrightness. Goethe agreed, observing that poets are forced by the conventions of the day to keep some of their best writing to themselves, and blaming this on the public's lack of true civilization—of 'intellect and superior culture' ('Geist und höhere Bildung'). But, he remarked, times change, and there may soon be a time in which poets can speak again with greater freedom. For time is

a whimsical tyrant, which in every century has a different face for all one says and does. We can no longer say with propriety things that were permitted to the ancient Greeks; and the Englishman of 1820 cannot endure what suited the vigorous contemporaries of Shakespeare, so that at the present day it is found necessary to have a Family Shakespeare.

It is sad to see how countless self-appointed guardians of Goethe's reputation, by bowing to the whimsical tyrant Convention, have fashioned for generations of readers just such a 'Family Goethe'.

Though written in Weimar, the *Roman Elegies* are essentially the fruit of Goethe's prolonged sojourn in Italy, from October 1786 to April 1788. Their title, like that of Rainer Maria Rilke's famous *Duino Elegies*, refers primarily to the place in which they were conceived.[11] Indeed, the *Roman Elegies* are inseparable from that locale, for it was in Rome that Goethe virtually re-invented himself as a poet—the poet now capable of writing these very *Elegies*.

Goethe was 37 when he determined to leave Germany for a while and to live in Italy—the land that had occupied his imagination since childhood, when he heard his father reminiscing about his own journey to Italy. Various mundane factors, but also psychological and cultural considerations, combined to lead Goethe simply to drop everything and seek fulfilment, as an artist and as a person, in the legendary 'land of art'. Undertaking this journey had become a matter of the utmost urgency. For eleven years he had devoted himself to his various social and administrative duties at the small ducal court of Weimar. Recently, though, he had begun to feel overburdened by the increasingly demanding responsibilities of his various ministerial offices; by the mounting tensions in his passion-

[11] See F. Beissner, *Geschichte der deutschen Elegie* (de Gruyter, 1941), 136; *Goethes Römische Elegien*, ed. D. Jost (Deutsche Klassik, 1974), 34.

ate but wholly platonic and, ultimately, unhealthy relationship with Charlotte von Stein, who was married; and last but not least by a growing sense of frustration in his more important literary endeavours, none of which, under the prevailing circumstances, he had been able to bring to fruition. Suddenly, at dawn on 3 September 1786, with the permission of Duke Karl August, his patron, but without informing his friends, Goethe left the Bohemian spa of Karlsbad, where he had spent the summer. Travelling hurriedly and in an almost perpetual state of exhilaration, he pressed on until, on 29 October, he arrived in Rome. After a four-month trip to Naples and Sicily, in the spring of 1787, he returned to Rome for another ten months; it was this second sojourn in the Eternal City that inspired him to write the *Roman Elegies*.

What made that celebrated journey such a liberating and consequential event in Goethe's life? In his own *Italian Journey*, written much later, we read chiefly about his observations of the landscape, his scientific speculations, his delight in architecture and painting, his joy in being at last on the 'classical soil' (Elegy VII) for which he had longed for so many years, and, again and again, about the lessons he learned as an artist and as a poet. The real if less publicized heart of the matter was something more intimate. Rome became the site of Goethe's sexual liberation. Whether he had suffered until then, as has been suggested, from a sexual disorder (*ejaculatio praecox*), which would have rendered him incapable of having proper intercourse,[12] or whether the social and moral pressures of his life had forced him to practise abstinence, however reluctantly, it is clear from all accounts we have that the post-Italian Goethe displayed, in word and in deed, a new and defiant attitude towards sexuality. Upon his return to Weimar his old friends noted, not always in a friendly spirit, that he had become sensual ('sinnlich') and had turned into a 'heathen'. In fact, what Goethe had accomplished was an admirably successful and lasting self-therapy; understandably, then, he never ceased to praise the time he spent in Italy as the happiest period of his life.

There has been a good deal of curiosity and speculation about the identity of Goethe's Roman mistress. From scattered hints we can

---

[12] On this point and on Goethe's sexual life in general see K. R. Eissler, *Goethe* (Wayne State University Press, 1963), 1058.

gather that she was a young widow (see Elegy VIII) who accepted the well-defined role of the *mantenuta*—the kept woman. Her interest in such a relationship is neatly summed up in Elegy IV:

Now she eats better than ever before, and has plenty of dresses;
    Drives to the opera now, fetched in an elegant coach.
Mother and daughter are pleased with their northern guest, and a Roman
    Bosom and body lie now under barbarian rule.

Obviously, the sexual service Goethe was enjoying came with a price-tag. We do not know how much this Roman sex clinic actually cost the poet, but it appears to have been a hefty sum. In a letter to Karl August (29 December 1787), his only confidant in sexual matters and himself a vigorous practitioner, Goethe characterized his financial conditions as tough ('böse Bedingungen'). Evidently they were not so tough, however, as to make him waver in his resolve to enjoy this adventure to the hilt.[13]

None the less, it would be wrong merely to read Goethe's poems as a faithful representation of his relationship with this shadowy Roman figure. For the lovers' idyll in the *Roman Elegies* is clearly a literary construct firmly anchored in mythology and the poetry of his chosen precursors. The name of the poet's beloved, 'Faustina', is itself one that marks her as the fictitious partner of an equally fictitious Faust. Ironically, Goethe was working on *Faust* at that very time; in fact, he wrote some of its most characteristically 'northern' scenes in Rome. Was the invention of the name 'Faustina' some sort of ironic recognition of his own 'Faustian' longings? After all, the Roman experience had in some sense satisfied one of Faust's essential desires, to 'embrace endless Nature', to suck at the very breasts of mother earth, as the earliest version of the text puts the matter, and to win the 'crown of our humanity'.[14]

As if to emphasize the gap between poetry and biographical truth, Goethe later had this to say to Eckermann (8 April 1829) about the public's apparently irrepressible curiosity regarding the 'facts' behind his *Roman Elegies*: 'People seldom reflect that a poet can generally make something good out of very little.'

We are on much safer ground with regard to a slightly later but related experience about which we know far more than we do about

---

[13] See F. Sengle, *Das Genie und sein Fürst* (Metzler, 1993).
[14] *Faust Part One*, tr. David Luke (World's Classics, 1987), ll. 455 ff., 1804.

the Roman affair: namely the beginning, soon after he returned to Weimar, of his long-lasting, affectionate, and fulfilling relationship with Christiane Vulpius. At the time of their meeting on 12 July 1788, Christiane, a woman from a middle-class background, was 23, an orphan and unmarried, and employed in a local manufactory of artificial flowers. Her brother Christian August Vulpius, then an impoverished writer, had asked her to present a petition to Goethe on his behalf. She did so as he was walking in the park outside his cottage by the River Ilm, in Weimar. It may well have been his self-liberating encounter with 'Faustina', in Rome, that enabled him to take the initiative that brought them together; at any rate, it appears that Goethe and Christiane became lovers on the very day of their first encounter.[15] Christiane lived with Goethe as his mistress until 1806, and then as his wife until her death in 1816. All Weimar was scandalized by this open liaison with a poorly educated young woman, who in the presence of company would address Goethe formally as 'Herr Privy Counsellor' and tactfully disappear. Among those especially offended was Charlotte, who never reconciled herself to her old friend's new domestic arrangements. But the relationship with Christiane, whom he called his 'little nature-creature' ('kleines Naturwesen'), became a lasting one in which, so far as we know, Goethe remained entirely faithful.[16] They had five children, of whom only the first, August (born 25 December 1789), survived infancy; August died in 1830, two years before his father.

It was in October of 1788, not long after he began to live with Christiane, that Goethe began to write the *Roman Elegies*: an imaginative and entirely convincing amalgam of Roman memories and a quite new present reality, enveloped in a pervasive, playfully woven web of intertextual allusions. Of Christiane's role in 'inspiring' this new poetry it has rightly been said that 'At the heart of the *Elegies* [. . .] there lies a completely happy experience such as we

---

[15] See E. Klessmann, *Christiane* (Artemis & Winkler, 1993), 11, 37 f.

[16] Judicious modern accounts of Goethe's relationship with Christiane appear in R. Friedenthal, *Goethe* (Weidenfeld & Nicolson, 1965), 254 ff., N. Boyle, *Goethe*, i (Clarendon Press, 1991), 537 ff., and Klessmann, *Christiane*. See also E. Beutler, 'Christiane', in *Essays um Goethe* (Dieterich'sche Verlagsbuchhandlung, 1948), Goethe's correspondence with Christiane (ed. H. G. Gräf, Ruetten & Loening, 1916) (in German), and his letters to Charlotte von Stein, ed. R. M. Browning (Camden House, 1990) (in English).

find in no other of Goethe's works [. . .] The literary complexities in which that central experience is enveloped should not lead us to overlook the biographical core.'[17] First in Rome and now in Weimar, Goethe had found a new source of strength and inspiration that he was determined to keep alive. Would he also be able to transfer to the northern world, with its gloomy skies and hostile moral climate, the kind of poetry he had envisioned under the ether of the South?

It is interesting to see the direction in which his new poetry now moved. In 'The Visit' ('Der Besuch') and 'Lament at Dawn' ('Morgenklagen'), two longish poems written in August 1788, Goethe painted two scenes of discreet, domestic eroticism. These otherwise unremarkable texts allow us to see clearly the dilemma confronting Goethe—or indeed any other poet at that time—with respect to erotic subjects. The choice was to use contemporary form with conventional subject matter, or daring subject matter in classical form. What was not permissible, it seems, was to be daring in an authentically modern idiom. Goethe therefore opted at this point for a poetic form (five-beat trochaic lines, and unrhymed stanzas of irregular length) which sounded contemporary, but which allowed no more than a restrained and conventional suggestion of sexuality.

He took an altogether different route in his *Roman Elegies*, a route that was to lead him much further in his project of creating a modern erotic poetry than the two preceding, conventional texts. If poetry was to speak of sexuality with the same honesty and depth that had been achieved in other realms of human experience, it had to disguise its voice. Already in 'The Visit' Goethe had taken up a classical motif from Propertius (the lover's contemplation of the sleeping beloved; cf. also Elegy XV). Now Propertius and, to a lesser extent, Tibullus and Catullus were to provide an intertextual matrix that could sustain and legitimize the naturalness and frankness Goethe was aiming at. By the same token, poetic speech also had to accommodate itself to the patterns and accents of the precursors. The *Roman Elegies* are founded on the realization that in

[17] Boyle, *Goethe*, i. 573. Boyle adds (p. 640): 'The *Elegies* are an immediate poetic response, of astonishing energy and novelty, to the most important event in [Goethe's] adult life after his move to Weimar in 1775, the establishment of a permanent relationship with Christiane Vulpius.'

modern times erotic poetry depended on classical form for its very survival. The elegiac distich that Goethe chose to adopt for this purpose proved, on the whole, effective enough in achieving the subtle distancing that was essential to the success of the undertaking.

Goethe must have intended to publish his *Elegies* soon after their completion in 1790. One of them (Elegy XV) appeared in a periodical in 1791. He was apparently contemplating publishing more, if not all of them, when he was advised against doing so by Karl August, as well as by Herder, the friend and mentor of his Storm and Stress days who was now an important church dignitary in Weimar. Goethe took their advice 'blindly', as he wrote (1 January 1791), somewhat resentfully, to his close friend Karl Ludwig von Knebel, and the *Elegies* were suppressed for several years. This of course appeared to imply a quite mistaken categorization of them as that kind of pornographic literary exercise which had to remain private. But the *Elegies* finally did appear in 1795, in Schiller's journal *Die Horen*. At Goethe's insistence their publication was anonymous, though his authorship quickly became an open secret.

Schiller's role in the literary fortunes of the *Elegies* turned out to be a crucial one. As with *Wilhelm Meister's Apprenticeship*, the traditional misreading of which as the classic idealistic *Bildungsroman* (novel of self-cultivation) was initiated by Schiller, his reading of the *Roman Elegies* left a lasting imprint on later generations of readers. Schiller was impressed by the poems, but one cannot overlook the fact that their 'liberty in the portrayal of Nature' caused him a certain amount of embarrassment. On first hearing the *Elegies* read to him by the author, he characterized them in a letter (14 September 1794) to his wife as '*risqué*, to be sure, and not very decent' ('zwar schlüpfrig und nicht sehr dezent'), but added that they belonged among the best of Goethe's works. In a letter (5 July 1795) to his patron the Duke of Schleswig-Holstein-Augustenburg, he defended their publication on the grounds of their 'lofty poetic beauty', adding that in his view 'they offend against a certain conventional decency, but not against that decency which is true and natural' ('die wahre und natürliche Dezenz'). This question of 'Dezenz' clearly troubled him; he therefore resolved to clarify the whole problem in a brief essay 'On the Modesty of Poets' ('Über die

Schamhaftigkeit der Dichter'). But instead of writing such an essay, he incorporated his thoughts on the matter into the famous treatise *On Naive and Reflective Poetry* (*Über naive und sentimentalische Dichtung*) (1797), Schiller's influential typological study of classical and modern literature. In that text, Schiller offers a generous appreciation and defence of Goethe's *Elegies*—but at a price.

Schiller clearly has the *Roman Elegies* in mind when he draws a distinction between the kind of erotic poetry that is 'objectionable' and 'vulgar' and a kind that is beautiful and noble. He argues forcefully that whenever the poet merely intends to titillate our desires, his work becomes empty, cold, and 'without question objectionable' ('verwerflich'). But he will produce something 'beautiful, noble, and praiseworthy in defiance of all frosty decency', if he can combine sophistication and emotion (literally 'mind and heart', 'Geist und Herz'), and if his writing is 'naïve'.[18] Herein lies the crux. The term 'naïve' in the Schillerian sense denotes 'in the spirit and manner of the ancients'. Schiller employs the term to differentiate between the essentially reflective, self-conscious manner of post-classical, modern literature, and the classical, essentially straightforward manner of the Greeks. It is difficult for us today to comprehend why Schiller would classify Goethe in general and the *Roman Elegies* in particular as examples of 'naïve' poetry. Goethe's poems are so obviously grounded in an awareness of his own historical distance from his Latin models that we wonder why Schiller chose this particular critical strategy. We may well speculate that he needed to set off his own, more philosophically inclined writing against Goethe's and thus justify it as different from, but of equal value to, the idealized model of poetic 'naïveté'.

Again, as in the case of *Wilhelm Meister's Apprenticeship*, Schiller's highly sophisticated reading of the *Roman Elegies* must, in the last analysis, be termed a misreading. Given Schiller's status in Goethe criticism generally, his characterization of Goethe's poems had far-reaching consequences. Perhaps its most problematic effect may be seen in the persistent tendency, especially in German criticism, to set Goethe somewhat apart from the mainstream of European Romanticism. This critical topos is largely responsible for the

---

[18] *Über naive und sentimentalische Dichtung*, tr. J. A. Elias (Frederick Ungar Publishing Co., 1966), 143 f.; tr. H. B. Nisbet (Cambridge University Press, 1985), 209.

failure to recognize the thoroughly modern and innovative mode of the *Roman Elegies*. It has also led to a failure to recognize the innovative tendency of Weimar Classicism in its imaginative endeavours as distinct from its aesthetic theories—a tendency of which Goethe's *Elegies* stand as perhaps the most representative example.

Most editions of Goethe's works present the *Roman Elegies* as a twenty-part cycle. This is the arrangement in which they were first published in 1795 under the title *Elegien: Rom, 1788*. There is considerable evidence, however, that this familiar arrangement, which Goethe authorized for posterity in the final edition of his works (*Ausgabe letzter Hand*), owes its order more to the dictates of convention and to self-censorship than, as some commentators have argued, to artistic considerations. It is important to know that Goethe had submitted to Schiller not twenty but twenty-two elegies for publication in *Die Horen*. After some discussion, he agreed to excise two of them altogether rather than to publish them in fragmentary form, with lines omitted, as Schiller had suggested. It is not entirely clear whether it was Goethe or Schiller who first considered dropping the two elegies. Given Schiller's initial ambivalence about their immodesty, we may assume that it was he who felt prompted to urge caution. In any case, he reported to his friend Körner (20 July 1795): 'The coarsest of Goethe's *Elegies* have been omitted, in order not to offend too much against decency.' We may also assume that Goethe consented out of concern for the well-being of the fledgeling journal and tact towards Schiller, who had only recently become his friend and ally.

The two excised elegies appear harmless enough and will hardly strike anyone today as offensive. In the first of them (no. III in the present edition), the splendour of Roman palaces is contrasted with the simplicity of the beloved's room. The poem concludes with a wonderfully resonant evocation of the pleasures of sexual union:

> Ours is the true, the authentic, the naked Love; and beneath us,
> Rocking in rhythm, the bed creaks the dear song of our joy.

The reasons for suppressing the other elegy (XVII) seem a little more persuasive. It speaks of the universally dreaded danger of

contracting venereal disease not only from a prostitute but also—
and this seems to have been the stumbling block—from one's own
wife:

> Who does not hesitate now to break faith with a tedious mistress?
>   Love may not hold us, but sheer caution will make us think twice.
> Even at home, who knows! Not a single pleasure is risk-free;
>   Who in his own wife's lap now lays a confident head?
> Neither in wedlock now nor out of it can we be certain;
>   Mutually noxious we are, husband and lover and wife.

To readers of today, dreading another 'new monster', these words
may seem more prophetic than Goethe could have suspected.

But even if these two elegies were restored to their proper place in
the cycle, as they are in some editions, we still could not claim to
know the *Roman Elegies* in their entirety and in the order in which
Goethe conceived them. Originally, the *Erotica Romana* were to
include two more elegies, making twenty-four in all. Both are cel-
ebrations of the phallic fertility-god Priapus, and for this reason
Goethe did not even bother to submit them to Schiller. The earthi-
ness and frankness traditionally associated with poetry in the
Priapean vein obviously disqualified them from publication. This,
however, should not obscure the fact that they represent a crucial
and, properly speaking, indispensable part of Goethe's project as a
whole.

Goethe was reading at that time not only the erotic poetry of the
classical 'triumvirate' but also the far less respectable *Carmina
Priapea*. These were a collection, or perhaps cycle, of about eighty
epigrammatic poems in honour of Priapus, dating from the first
century AD.[19] They had enjoyed a certain underground currency
throughout the centuries, especially among the sixteenth-century
Humanists. It is clear that Goethe had more than a nodding ac-
quaintance with these poems. He studied them in the winter of

---

[19] A distinguished modern edition is available (*Priapea: Poems for a Phallic God*, ed.
W. H. Parker, Croom Helm, 1988) complete with verse translation and scholarly
apparatus. The identity of the author or authors of the poems is uncertain, but see also
V. Buchheit, *Studien zum Corpus Priapeorum* (Beck, 1962), who argues persuasively
(pp. 19 ff.) for their cyclical organization and for a single authorship. The *Priapea* also
appear in a Latin and German bilingual edition (*Gedichte an den Gartengott*, ed.
B. Kytzler, tr. C. Fischer, Artemis, 1978). A pseudonymous English translation
(*Priapeia; or The Sportive Epigrams of Divers Poets on Priapus*, tr. 'Neaniskos') was
privately printed in 1890.

1789/90 in a seventeenth-century edition furnished with learned commentaries by Renaissance scholars,[20] and wrote his own learned comments on nine of the poems, emulating his predecessors by proposing textual emendations. His commentary—in Latin, of course—was addressed to 'Princeps Augustus', which probably refers to Duke Karl August of Weimar, who savoured such writings and was a frequent recipient of Goethe's sexual confidences.[21] Analysing Goethe's essay on the *Priapea*, Kurt R. Eissler has rightly observed that it

explores topics of intense emotional value. Under the guise of philology the forbidden and the obscene are brought to light and made the subject of communication. This combination of dry objectivity with the indecent makes the charm of these seemingly casual compositions. Psychologically, however, they are not as casual as their author wishes to make it appear. [...] He was fascinated by the subject like someone who has started to fathom its full meaning and now cannot wrest his mind from his interest in it.[22]

This personal, biographical motif notwithstanding, Goethe's reading of the *Priapea* must be viewed as part of his work on the *Elegies*. He himself explained as much in his introductory remarks to the Duke:

It is not vouchsafed to man, as it is to the sparrows, to enjoy Venus continually, and many men join with [Caspar] Schoppe in deploring this circumstance. But I have always, most excellent Prince, been of a mind not anxiously to yearn for what chance has denied me, and accordingly I have always endeavored to fill out with some useful or agreeable occupation the intervals by which Nature has separated my pleasures. On the same principle I have also been amusing myself, in the long nights of this winter which is now drawing to a close, by passing them alternately with Venus and with the more indulgent Muses.[23]

[20] *Priapeia, sive diversorum poetarum in Priapum lusus* (1664), with commentaries by Caspar Schoppe and Joseph Scaliger. Goethe had his own copy of this classic edition, bound in one volume with Petronius' *Satyricon*.

[21] It is also possible, however, that the dedicatee was Prince August (1747–1806), a younger brother of Duke Ernst II of Saxe-Gotha-Altenburg. August of Gotha was an enlightened and cultivated bachelor, a connoisseur of Latin poetry, who knew Herder, Goethe, and other members of the Weimar circle.

[22] Eissler, *Goethe*, 1340 f.

[23] Moses Hadas's English translation of Goethe's essay (here quoted with slight alterations) is given in full ibid. 1332 ff.

The pages on some of the *Priapea* which he enclosed with these remarks were meant to testify to the more pleasurable of his nocturnal activities.

Reading and writing erotic poetry had indeed become more pleasurable to Goethe that winter. It was the time of Christiane's first pregnancy. On 25 December 1789 she gave birth to August, only survivor of their five children. Goethe's reference to the 'more indulgent Muses' clearly implies some creative work—not just his reading of the *Priapea* but his writing of *erotica* in general. Quite obviously he presents his interest in Priapean poetry as part of his work on the *Roman Elegies*; for this reason alone, Goethe's own Priapean elegies should be considered an inseparable part of the larger project.

One cannot help feeling somewhat baffled by the strange configuration of interests that dominated Goethe's thoughts in the winter of 1789/90. Shortly after the outbreak of the Revolution in France, which he observed with the greatest apprehension and which turned into *the* political trauma of his life, he devoted a great deal of time to what appears to be an entirely unconnected activity: the creation of a poetry born from a most private 'revolution' in his own sexual life. Or is there a hidden connection?

Without wishing to press the matter unduly, one is in fact tempted to see a parallel, however sketchy, between the radicalism of the events unfolding in France and the radicalism of Goethe's attempt to liberate German poetry from the tyranny of certain conventions. In the light of this correspondence, his preoccupation with Priapus and Priapean poetry assumes a new significance beyond the obviously psychological one. The ancient deity of fertility, traditionally depicted with an outsize wooden penis, represented the low, popular strata of the culture of antiquity.[24] This is certainly true of the early Greek monuments documenting the cult of Priapus and

---

[24] It may be significant that Sir William Hamilton, a wealthy connoisseur who was British ambassador to Naples at the time of Goethe's Italian journey, was interested in the cult of Priapus and had contributed an essay to an erotically illustrated book on the subject (Richard Payne Knight, *Account of the Remains of the Worship of Priapus*, published privately in 1786). We know from the *Italian Journey* that when staying in Naples in 1787 Goethe was on friendly visiting terms with Hamilton and his young mistress Emma Hart (later Lady Hamilton), and was shown his collection of artistic curiosities. It is thus possible that the contact with Hamilton was a contributory stimulus to Goethe's Priapic studies.

of the Roman *Priapea* of the first century AD, which represent a late, parodistic stage of the cult. Goethe clearly wanted to reach back to these popular and coarser elements of erotic poetry. Did he believe that the creation of truly liberated poetry was predicated on recovering the phallic deity? Or was he guided by an intuitive understanding of the centrality of the phallus in human sexuality—thereby anticipating a central aspect of Freud? We cannot be sure. What we can say with certainty is that the resurrection of Priapus in Elegies I and XXIV epitomizes the decidedly anti-Christian emphasis of the *Roman Elegies*.

The official, technical term for the activity celebrated in Goethe's poems is fornication—a grave sin. In the language of the Church, all sexual gratification outside marriage was sinful; and even in marriage, the limits of sex were carefully circumscribed in view of the divine injunction to procreate. But as Michel Foucault has shown, it was precisely the official stance of the Church with its highly knowledgeable and sophisticated discourse on sexuality, dating from the early Church Fathers, that paradoxically spurred and deepened the awareness of sexuality.[25] The moral teachings of the Christian churches by no means eliminated the need for erotic poetry. They helped rather to sharpen the focus. This is less evident in the *Roman Elegies*, with its two unmarried lovers, than it is in *The Diary*, where by choosing a married protagonist Goethe focused more clearly on the fundamental Christian concepts governing sexual activity.

In the first of Goethe's Priapean poems, the poet develops a stock motif of the *Priapea* and appoints Priapus as the guardian of his own 'garden', which here of course stands for the *Elegies* themselves. Anyone is welcome to help himself to the golden fruit of life that grows here: Priapus is also instructed to punish with his mighty instrument all 'miscreants' who may come to defile the garden and all 'hypocrites' who would express disgust at the 'fruits of pure nature'. This short poem has an unmistakable introductory function.

In the other, somewhat longer poem, Priapus himself speaks: he gives thanks to the 'honest' poet for having rescued him from neglect and abuse and for having restored him to his rightful place

[25] See M. Foucault, *A History of Sexuality*, i (Penguin, 1979).

among the gods—a vindication accomplished through the *Roman Elegies*. As a reward Priapus promises the poet the joys of fabulous sexual potency:

> Therefore I bless your magnificent central rod, may it always
> Stand up half a foot tall at your beloved's behest.
> May your member not tire, until you have both done the dozen
> Figures Philaenis describes, finished the dance of your joy.

It is not difficult to see the structural function of these two Priapean elegies: they are clearly meant to form a frame for the other twenty-two.[26] Even though the extant manuscripts offer no clear indication of a twenty-four-part arrangement, there is indeed much indirect evidence, as Karl Otto Conrady has noted, supporting this assumption.[27] Such a framing device is quite in keeping with the structure of the *Carmina Priapea*, which display several such framings.[28] In the opening poem of the *Roman Elegies*, the 'prologue', where one would traditionally expect an invocation of the Muses or of Venus, Goethe calls instead upon Priapus as the true genius of the poetry that is to follow. And the other Priapean elegy, the 'epilogue', reveals and confirms the secret mission of the *Elegies*: the recovery and vindication of Priapus.

It may be recalled here that the theme of recovery—of rehabilitation or 'Rettung'—is fundamental to Goethe's literary identity. Many of his early literary projects were undertaken with the express intent of recovering a historical or mythical figure from neglect or opprobrium. This applies for instance to the historical drama *Götz von Berlichingen* (1771), to the narrative poem *Hans Sachs's Poetic Mission* (1776), and above all to *Faust* (begun in the early 1770s), which carries the idea of 'Rettung' (literally 'saving') to its most far-reaching implications. In the *Roman Elegies*, this fundamental gesture of recovery is focused on Priapus. And as in the other cases, the recovery of the deposed and abused phallic god may be viewed as an act of liberation—liberation, that is, from outdated and unproductive paradigms of erotic poetry.

[26] As far as I have been able to ascertain, Harry G. Haile (*Boston University Journal*, 27, 1979) is the only previous translator of the *Roman Elegies* to present the complete twenty-four-part cycle in the appropriate order, i.e. with the two Priapean poems as a frame.

[27] See K. O. Conrady, *Goethe* (Athenäum, 1982), 522.

[28] See Buchheit, *Studien*, 40 ff.

It will now be obvious that any reading of the *Roman Elegies* will be significantly affected once we have accepted the Priapean frame as an integral part of the cycle. The two Priapean texts reinforce the importance of the allusion in Elegy XIII, at the centre of the cycle, to the phallic god, the 'glorious son' of Dionysus and Aphrodite. Likewise, the 'Gott' invoked at the conclusion of Elegy XXI can only be Priapus, or rather Love in its priapic incarnation. Furthermore, the two secreted framing poems lead us to identify the 'genius' invoked at the beginning of Elegy II as Priapus. He, and not some vague *genius loci* as most commentators seem to think, is the true genius of the *Roman Elegies*. Instead of centring the cycle's poetic aim on some vaguely felt interplay of present and past, or of 'Roma' and 'Amor', we can now define it more confidently and precisely as the recovery of Priapus, who is present, explicitly and implicitly, in the *Elegies* as a whole.

This makes it understandable why so many commentators have been eager to separate the Priapean poems from the main body of the *Elegies*. Apparently they feared—and not without reason—that the entire corpus of elegies, whose 'moral' character had to be maintained at all cost, might be spoiled or rendered unpalatable by a sort of Priapean pollution.

This kind of resistance to Priapus has by no means been restricted to older practices of literary criticism. In the early literature, preconceived notions about Goethe's work in general and about the design of the *Roman Elegies* in particular kept Priapus out of the discussion; today, ambitious theoretical agendas are more likely to be the undoing of the phallic god. Predictably, the *Elegies* have been subjected to a thoroughly deconstructive reading, in which the lover-poet of the *Elegies* is discovered to be 'a passive lover whose passion is greater for literature and literary fame' than it is 'for life'. The fact that Goethe published only twenty elegies, and thereby 'truncated' the total corpus of poems, is said to be indicative, somehow, of a fundamentally 'emasculated sexuality'.[29] Here, the separation of the two Priapean elegies is presented as sign of a diminished notion of sexuality, as though the decision to omit them was dictated not by external factors but by some inner necessity. Obviously, as soon as

---

[29] K. D. Weisinger, *The Classical Façade* (Pennsylvania State University Press, 1988), 23, 168.

the original twenty-four-part conception of the *Elegies* is acknowledged, such readings lose all credibility. In an even more fanciful reading it has been suggested that the sexual acts represented in the *Elegies* are but thinly disguised practices of 'mutual masturbation', and that the entire work, but especially the famous Elegy VII (in which the poet is tapping hexameters on his lover's back), is encoded with signs of a homoerotic, Winckelmannian sensibility.[30] Here too, the pervasive Priapean theme of the *Elegies* is simply ignored. Priapus is felt to be an irritant, and that in itself, it seems, calls for his deconstruction.

In the last analysis, the Priapean frame of the *Roman Elegies*, beyond its obvious role as a sexual marker, serves a specifically aesthetic function. It alerts the reader from the outset to the basically ironic posture of a work that mediates playfully between the rampant paganism of the fiction and the entirely Christian consciousness of the implied reader. This irony is often overlooked, as is, concomitantly, what may be considered the most distinctive and innovative feature of Goethe's erotic poetry: its self-conscious reflection on the dilemma of the modern erotic poet. Such self-referentiality surfaces even more insistently twenty years later in that other monument of Goethe's erotic poetry, *The Diary*.

The group of brief poems known as *Venetian Epigrams* can hardly be counted among Goethe's major poetic statements. Most commentators treat the collection as decidedly minor—the idle pastime of one of the poet's more sour moods. The *Venetian Epigrams* may indeed be 'Goethe's least read and least appreciated work'.[31] This is a pity, for they are of considerable interest in and for themselves. What is more, they are indispensable to any serious consideration of Goethe's erotic poetry as a whole, even though only a limited number of them can be said to have an explicitly erotic content.

Characteristically, it was Nietzsche who, demonstrating a fine appreciation of the unsentimental flavour and iconoclastic thrust of these epigrams, came to their defence. He did so at the time of his no-holds-barred attack on Richard Wagner for having become

---

[30] S. Gilman, *Inscribing the Other* (University of Nebraska Press, 1991), 45 ff.

[31] M. K. Flavell, 'The Limits of Truth-Telling', *Oxford German Studies*, 12 (1981), 39.

a traitor to the cause of erotic and sexual liberation in his final work, *Parsifal*. For Nietzsche, the case of Goethe was an instructive precedent to that of his immediate concern, *The Case of Wagner*:

We know what Goethe's fate has been in moraline-sour, old-maidish Germany. Germans have always found him offensive, his only honest admirers have been Jewesses. Schiller, 'noble' Schiller who lambasted the ears of the Germans with big words—*he* was a man after their own hearts. What did they hold against Goethe? The 'Venusberg', and the fact that he had written Venetian epigrams. [. . .] There was a time when Herder liked to use the word Priapus whenever he spoke of Goethe. [. . .] But above all, the higher virgins were indignant: every petty court, every 'Wartburg'[32] in Germany— they all crossed themselves against Goethe, against the 'unclean spirit' in Goethe.[33]

It is clear from this that Nietzsche saw in Goethe a fellow 'free spirit' and felt that much of this free spirit had found expression—concise, irreverent, and, at times, aggressive expression—in the *Venetian Epigrams*.

All or almost all of the 'Epigramme: Venedig 1790', as they were first named, were written in Venice between 11 March and 22 May 1790, during Goethe's brief second Italian journey. He went there reluctantly on the official business of meeting and attending Karl August's mother, who was returning from an extended tour of Italy. The Dowager Duchess's arrival was repeatedly delayed, however, and the attractions of Venice evidently failed to compensate for Goethe's homesickness for Christiane and baby August, their first-born, back in Weimar. Under these circumstances it was perhaps inevitable that he should experience this unexpected return trip to Italy as a disappointment, as something of a personal anticlimax. Painfully, he had to admit that the land he remembered as Arcadia had lost its enchantment. In a letter to the Duke (3 April 1790) he even went so far as to declare that the present trip had dealt a death-blow to his love for Italy. Needless to say, such an ill-tempered pronouncement proved to be a vast exaggeration.

There is no denying, however, that the *Venetian Epigrams* reflect a mood of disillusionment. They also lack the kind of thematic focus

[32] In Act II of Wagner's *Tannhäuser*, the 'Wartburg' is associated with moral complacency and intolerance.

[33] See F. Nietzsche, *The Birth of Tragedy* and *The Case of Wagner*, tr. W. Kaufmann (Vintage Books, 1967), 161 ff. The translation has here been slightly revised.

that shaped the cycle of *Roman Elegies*. The most one could say is
that variety itself has become a theme. On the other hand, whatever
the *Epigrams* may lack in coherence and design is amply compen-
sated by their spirit of uninhibited curiosity and by their freshness
of observation. It almost seems as though Goethe had been waiting
to seize the opportunity of this unexpectedly prolonged sojourn in
Venice to revive the mordant, Mephistophelian strain of his sensi-
bility that had been dormant, and in danger of withering, in the
stifling atmosphere of propriety and restraint at the court of
Weimar. Here, away from home, Goethe learned to speak, again, in
a voice that would deliberately transgress the conventional bound-
aries of government, religion, and morality—of 'Staat, Götter und
Sitten'. It was in Venice, then, at a time of mounting concern over
the potential fall-out from the Revolution in France, that the 40-
year-old poet regained some of his independence as an observer of
contemporary life and with it some of his self-awareness as a free-
thinker in the Nietzschean sense.

Making a virtue out of his mood of disillusionment, Goethe
adopted the perspective of the detached, ironic observer, very much
in the manner of the *flâneur* whom Walter Benjamin was to identify
as an emblematically modern type.[34] And indeed, as Wolfdietrich
Rasch has pointed out, Goethe's voyeuristic observations of
Venetian city life prefigure the fascination that later poets such as
Heine, Baudelaire, and Rilke experienced in Paris. The clearest
indication of this is provided by the appearance in the *Epigrams* of
the figure of the 'Gaukler', the travelling acrobat and street enter-
tainer. Goethe's Venetian acrobats belong to the same type of
'saltimbanques' that, about a hundred years later, achieved such a
privileged status in the iconography of modernism in the work of
Picasso, Rilke, and others.[35]

Evidently, Goethe came upon such a group of street performers;
their leader was the father of an adolescent female acrobat, here
named Bettina. If there is a central sequence within the *Venetian
Epigrams*, it is this mini-cycle of fifteen or so short poems celebrat-
ing the gymnastic artistry of Bettina, who appears capable of achiev-

---

[34] W. Benjamin, *Reflections*, tr. E. Jephcott (Harcourt Brace Jovanovich, 1978),
156 ff.
[35] See W. Rasch, 'Die Gauklerin Bettine', in S. A. Corngold *et al.* (eds.), *Aspekte der
Goethezeit* (Vandenhoek & Ruprecht, 1977), 115 ff.

ing anything from a breath-taking *salto mortale* to a self-performed cunnilingus. There is no hint here, of course, of any emotional involvement on the part of the poet. But there is more than a touch of the *flâneur*'s delighted appreciation of street life, as Goethe highlights the epicene charms of Bettina which recall the ambiguous gender of Wilhelm Meister's Mignon, and as he plays with the intriguing affinity between the juggler and the poet—the 'Gaukler und Dichter'.

Bettina's artful display is but one of several themes that provided Goethe with the occasion to indulge his penchant for religious and sexual iconoclasm. That penchant was still as keen as it had been in his early years and produced some memorable blasphemies (19, 28, 29). The *Venetian Epigrams* mark the site of what is perhaps the most violent clash in all Goethe's work between bourgeois-Christian convention and pagan Priapean sensibility; they constitute one of his most aggressively anti-Christian gestures.

There could, of course, be no thought of going public with the entire harvest of his Venetian sojourn. When in 1796 Goethe put together a collection of 103 epigrams for publication (again anonymously) in Schiller's *Musenalmanach*, he exercised some prophylactic self-censorship, as in the case of the *Roman Elegies* the previous year, and withheld fifty-three of the most offensive epigrams. And what a well-advised precaution that was, for they treat, as Nicholas Boyle lists them, such 'unacceptable subjects as nudity, erection, masturbation, both male and female (the latter also oral), prostitution, sodomy, venereal disease, and the disappointments of a loose vagina, compared to a Venetian canal'.[36] None the less, it has to be acknowledged that the fifty-three items that were excised owe their existence to the same impetus that triggered the other, less offensive epigrams. They must be considered an integral part of the collection, just as the two Priapean elegies cannot be separated from the *Roman Elegies*. In their almost casual aggressiveness, they reveal the true measure of Goethe's free spirit.

The *Venetian Epigrams*—those that Goethe published and those he withheld—are marked, and perhaps marred, by some vehemently anticlerical invective—something that surfaces whenever Goethe dons his Priapean mask and speaks on behalf of the exiled

[36] Boyle, *Goethe*, i. 660.

ancient god. That he should do so here is all the more remarkable, since, unlike the Roman cycle, the *Epigrams* were occasioned by no erotic adventure in the conventional sense. To the extent that the *Venetian Epigrams* are shaped by an experience in the emphatic Goethean sense, they rather echo and reflect the new-found self-confidence that was the result of his liaison with Christiane. If Goethe felt impelled here to pursue any Priapean agenda at all, it must have been out of a self-consciously poetic interest, rather than any urgently personal impulse. What we can observe here is a poet striving to reclaim for Priapus the space that he should rightfully occupy in the pantheon of German poetry. In this regard, the *Venetian Epigrams* hark back to the *Roman Elegies* and foreshadow *The Diary*: they continue the reflection on the plight of the modern erotic poet, and they pave the way, as it were, for that most defiant and offensive of gestures in all of Goethe's work—the direct confrontation between the crucified god of Christianity and the indomitable Priapus himself.

Clearly, this 'least read and least appreciated' work of Goethe's provides a bridge between the *Roman Elegies* and *The Diary*: indeed, it reveals both the scope and the inner coherence of Goethe's Priapean project as a whole.

The publication history of *The Diary* is even more curious than that of the *Elegies* or of the *Venetian Epigrams*.[37] Again we have a case of self-censorship. Goethe wrote *The Diary*, or rather finished it, in April 1810, and all the evidence suggests that he regarded it as a poem of some importance, but one which it would be impossible to publish. He thus consigned it, with other 'impossible' texts such as the Satanic Mass intended for the 'Walpurgis Night' section in *Faust*, to what he called his 'Walpurgis sack'.[38] He did, however, enjoy reading it aloud or showing it to various friends. Only two manuscripts of the poem appear to have survived: one in the hand of Friedrich Wilhelm Riemer (Goethe's resident philological adviser and the private tutor of his son August) with emendations in

[37] See S. Unseld, *'Das Tagebuch' Goethes und Rilkes 'Sieben Gedichte'* (Insel, 1978), 70 ff.
[38] See A. Schöne, *Götterzeichen, Liebeszauber und Satanskult* (Beck, 1981), 197 f., 210 f.; D. Borchmeyer, 'Die geheimgehaltenen Dichtungen des Geheimrats Goethe', in Wittkowski (ed.), *Verlorene Klassik?*

INTRODUCTION XXXV

Goethe's own hand, and another copy by someone unknown.[39] An original autograph seems to have existed but it has never been found. *The Diary* was first published in 1861, in a privately printed, limited edition, by the Berlin bookdealer Salomon Hirzel, but just how the text of the poem found its way into the hands of Hirzel is not entirely clear. This first printing, based on what Hirzel believed to be Goethe's autograph, was the beginning of a whole series of under-the-counter special editions in which the poem regularly surfaced from its literary limbo for the next century or so. As was perhaps to be expected, the text has usually been read simply as a thinly veiled and altogether embarrassing confession by the 60-year-old Goethe of an extramarital encounter thwarted by impotence.

In 1885, when the great Weimar edition of Goethe's works was in preparation under the patronage of Karl August's granddaughter-in-law the Grand Duchess Sophia,[40] its editors submitted the contents of the 'Walpurgis sack' to the patroness. Her Royal Highness, we are told, spent an evening with her ladies-in-waiting reading *The Diary* and the unpublished *Venetian Epigrams* aloud, and scratching words out with penknives; most have since been restored. She then decreed that all this material should continue to be withheld from publication. It was not until 1910, thirteen years after the Grand Duchess's death, that prudery was so far overcome by scholarly scruple as to permit the editors to include Hirzel's (corrupt) text of the poem in an obscure supplementary volume, hidden away among the text-critical apparatus.[41] But even here, the two most daring and notorious lines in the poem (135 f.) were partly deleted and were not restored until 1914, buried even more obscurely in a list of variant readings.[42] Since then, the correct or nearly correct text has been properly included in the best complete editions of Goethe's works, but the whole poem is shunned in almost all anthologies, and even

[39] For a more complete discussion of the philological evidence see H. Sachse, 'Textkritisches zu den Drucken von Goethes Gedicht "Das Tagebuch"', *Goethe-Jahrbuch*, 96 (1979), 291 ff.; H. R. Vaget, *Goethe* (Athenäum, 1982), 29 ff.; K. Eibl (ed.), *Goethes sämtliche Werke*, Gedichte ii (Insel, 1988), 1324.

[40] The WA (see Bibliography 1) was the first and is still the most complete and authoritative historical-critical edition of Goethe's entire literary output, scientific writings, diaries, and letters; its 143 volumes were published from 1887 to 1919.

[41] WA v/ii. 325 ff.

[42] WA liii. 562.

large scholarly multi-volume selections (such as the commonly used Hamburg edition by Erich Trunz) refrain from including *The Diary*. Special private printings of the poem on its own, however, continue unabated to this day, often furnished with frivolous and misleading illustrations. The first English translation (in prose) appeared in David Luke's bilingual selection of Goethe's verse (Penguin, 1964); the first English verse rendering was attempted by John Frederick Nims and published in 1968 in *Playboy Magazine*.

The Diary unfolds a carefully organized narrative that centres on the failure of an older man in a sexual encounter with a young woman. Poets have only rarely turned to this subject matter, and when they did the intent was, by and large, to ridicule the whole episode. Three notable examples of this motif may be found in Ovid's *Amores* (3. 7), in Ariosto's *Orlando Furioso* (8. 46 ff.), and in *The Imperfect Enjoyment*, a poem by John Wilmot, Earl of Rochester (1647–80).[43] Goethe seems not to have known Rochester's poem, but he was familiar with Ariosto's work from his youth and of course knew Ovid. But although both texts treat the same motif of sexual failure, the situation is in both cases quite different from that in Goethe's poem. In Ovid, the failure befalls a young man, and his partner—an older, more experienced woman—pretends to have succeeded in having intercourse all the same in order to avoid being teased by her female friends. The protagonist in Ariosto's episode is a lecherous old hermit who attempts to rape the sleeping Angelica. There are some faint echoes of these two earlier examples in Goethe's poem, but they play no significant part in it.

A much more likely and fruitful point of departure was provided by his own *Roman Elegies*. There, in the concluding Priapean elegy, the poet was promised unfailing sexual potency as a reward for the labour of love by which he had restored Priapus. Here the same poet, disguised only thinly as a diary-writing travelling merchant, reflects explicitly on the inexplicable failure of his supposedly fail-safe gift from Priapus. In view of this, Goethe could conceivably have been prompted to revoke the recovery of Priapus accomplished in the *Elegies*. But the poem proposes nothing of the sort.

[43] J. Wilmot, Earl of Rochester, *Complete Poems*, ed. D. M. Vieth (Yale University Press, 1968), 37 ff.

Further connections between the two texts can easily be detected. Like the *Elegies* in their original design, *The Diary* exhibits a twenty-four-part structure. The later poem also employs a framing device similar to that of the *Elegies*, and its structure displays an equally pronounced symmetry. Goethe obviously knew Eros well enough to realize that its natural lawlessness called for the discipline of form and the imposition of fairly rigid aesthetic laws. In both works, Goethe uses the same constellation of figures—a travelling writer and a young woman—thereby setting the stage for the central concern of both texts, though more explicitly of *The Diary*: namely, to reflect on the intimate interdependence of the act of love and the act of writing as the two exemplary manifestations of human creativity. In the *Roman Elegies* (VII), this theme was immortalized in the motif of the poet tapping the rhythm of the hexameter on his beloved's back:

> Often I even compose my poetry in her embraces,
>   Counting hexameter beats, tapping them out on her back
> Softly, with one hand's fingers.

Goethe explores the relationship of writing to the love act more confidently in *The Diary* by focusing on the failure of both sexual and artistic powers—the one mirroring and illuminating the other.

The Diary reflects with great clarity a particular dilemma in which the modern poet finds himself: the absence of an established canon of poetic forms adequate to the needs of erotic poetry. In the important conversation of 25 February 1824 already cited, Goethe and Eckermann went on to discuss the 'mysterious and great effects produced by the different poetical forms'. Goethe observed that the *Roman Elegies*, had they been written 'in the style and metre of Byron's *Don Juan*', would be found 'quite infamous'. By the same token Eckermann would have preferred to see *The Diary* written in a classical metre. This, he felt, would have distanced it from contemporary reality. As it stood, the form of the poem did not provide the necessary veil of modesty for it to be allowed out into decent society. Clearly, it was not the subject matter of the poem but its form that troubled Eckermann. He was especially troubled by the fact that *The Diary* treated an erotic adventure 'of our day in the language of our day'. But does the poem in fact employ the poetic idiom of 1810? There is no simple answer to this question. The vocabulary is unmistakably contemporary, hardly distinguishable from that of Goethe's novel *Die Wahlverwandtschaften* (*Elective Affinities*) (1809), its immediate neighbour chronologically. The use of *ottava rima*, on the other hand, does seem to hark back to an older poetic mode. What exactly is the function of this particular stanza form? And why would Goethe choose for *The Diary* the very form that would have made his *Roman Elegies* sound 'infamous'?

Don Juan could not, of course, be the model for the poetic form of Goethe's poem since it antedates Byron's work by some ten years. Rather, they both look back to the same great model of all modern writing in *ottava rima*, the *Orlando Furioso* of 'Meister Ariost' as Eckermann calls him. And this throws into relief a basic dilemma of modern poetry: the disparity between the contemporary experience of the erotic and the historical modes of erotic writing on which the poet, for lack of a continuous tradition, is obliged to rely. In *The Diary*, such a disparity can clearly be felt between the thoroughly contemporary flavour of the erotic adventure and the historical garb in which it is clad, between the 'naturalism' of the theme and the stateliness and elaborate splendour of its form.

Given the rather rigid technical requirements of *ottava rima*, it is not surprising that Goethe used it only sparingly and on special occasions. It is therefore all the more instructive to note for what kind of text he did use it. One immediately thinks of 'Orphic Primal Words' ('Urworte: Orphisch') (1817) with its profound reflections on individual destiny, chance, love, necessity, and hope—each theme concentrated into the eight lines of a single stanza; or of the moving commemorative poem about Schiller, 'Epilogue to Schiller's Song of the Bell' ('Epilog zu Schillers Glocke') (1805). Other examples are 'The Mysteries' ('Die Geheimnisse'), a puzzling, symbolic epic begun in 1784 but which remained a fragment, and especially the two poems called 'Dedication' ('Zueignung'): the first (1784) originally intended as a prologue to 'The Mysteries' and one of Goethe's great self-assessments as a poet, and the other (1797) also reflecting on his life and poetic career at the time of resuming the composition of *Faust* and standing as a 'dedicatory' prologue to his *magnum opus*. The company of such personal and esoteric poems provides a somewhat surprising but illuminating context for *The Diary*. It seems to indicate that this poem, too, speaks of something mysterious and profound, as do all of his other texts in this particular form.

We know that, aside from Ariosto, Goethe had another, more recent Italian model in mind: the enormously successful *Novelle galanti in ottave rime* by the Abbate Giambattista Casti. Goethe had made the acquaintance of this clerical author in Rome, where he heard him recite one of his verse novellas, *L'Arcivescovo di Praga*. Goethe found it 'slightly improper but extraordinarily well written in *ottava rima*'.[44] Not surprisingly, he refreshed his memory of Casti's writing when he himself, in August of 1808, contemplated a not so respectable subject matter for a *novella galante* of sorts.

It appears that the idea for *The Diary* first occurred to him during the early stages of his work on *Elective Affinities*. He returned to it after the completion of the novel and actually wrote the poem in 1810. This suggests that the idea of *The Diary* was in his mind during the whole of the intense period in which he composed *Elective Affinities*. A startling configuration indeed, especially in view of the thematic affinities between the two works![45] The novel, as well as the poem, is about marriage and about an adultery which both happens and does not happen. At the centre of both works we find a psychological situation in which the libido is aroused by an absent object of desire rather than by the present partner. But the two texts stand at opposite poles in their manner of resolving this situation: in the novel its consequences are inexorably tragic, whereas *The Diary*, as we shall see, proposes a conciliatory resolution. The poem may thus be viewed as a corrective afterthought, as it were, with which Goethe sought to restore the balance that had been upset by the tragic force of the novel.

Casti's novellas treat erotic anecdotes in conventionally veiled form and provide the reader with a rather predictable moral. In *The Diary* Goethe appears to be toying with this convention of the genre. He places in the foreground the kind of erotic adventure one would expect to find in a *novella galante*, and he does offer a rather comforting moral. Or so it seems. But can we be sure that the poem in fact offers precisely the kind of moral the reader has been led to expect?

---

[44] Goethe, *Italian Journey*, Suhrkamp edn., vi. 293.
[45] See T. J. Reed, *Goethe* (Oxford University Press, 1984), 86 f.

A married man of mature years, returning from a business trip, is forced to spend an additional night on the road because of a broken carriage-wheel. He is a writer of sorts who is in the habit, when absent from his wife, of recording his day's doings every night in a diary which he keeps for their mutual pleasure. At the inn he encounters an irresistibly attractive servant-girl. That night, inexplicably, he is quite unable to write the usual fluent entries in his diary. It turns out that he is also incapable of making love to the girl, who has joined him in his room, desirous of making him her first lover. Thrown into despair by his unexpected impotence, and lying awake next to the girl, he begins to recall in loving detail the untroubled pleasures of making love in his youth with the young woman who became and still is his wife. He remembers with particular vividness their wedding and the wedding ceremony—and this sets the stage for one of the most provocative gestures in all of Goethe, the confrontation of the crucifix and the erect male sexual organ.

> And when at last we wed, I do confess
> Before that altar and that priest, before
> Thy wretched bloodstained cross, *domine Christe*,
> God pardon me! it stirred and rose, my *iste*. (ll. 133–6)

This was the particular passage of which the exact wording was not revealed in print until 1914. From the way the offending last couplet—in all the older printings of the poem and indeed for more than a century since Goethe wrote it—was editorially mutilated or simply expunged altogether, we may conclude that the provocative intention of this climactic stanza was widely recognized. The juxtaposition of the phallus and the central symbol of Christianity could hardly be viewed otherwise than as an openly defiant, polemical gesture by a 'decided non-Christian' ('dezidierter Nicht-Christ'), as Goethe liked to call himself.

Goethe was painfully aware of the difficulty of naming the penis in German. Precisely this difficulty of finding an acceptable German word for that indispensable requisite of the mature and uninhibited poetry he sought to write had prompted him earlier to a notorious Venetian epigram in Priapean vein (no. 9) which remained unpublished, with many others, for over a century. In *The Diary*, the word chosen for 'der Schwanz' was 'der Iste'—to rhyme with 'Christe'. It is the personified Latin demonstrative pronoun, meaning something like 'this thing here'. There has been some speculation about the origin and function of this curious lexical choice. But given the hieratic context, and in view of the central role assigned to the phallic god in the *Roman Elegies*, we may very well read the word 'Iste' as metonymy—*pars pro toto*—for Priapus himself. A similarly blasphemous juxtaposition of the crucifix and Priapus, the god 'from Lampsacus' on the Hellespont (where his cult supposedly originated), occurs in another (no. 28) of the secreted *Epigrams*: a display of bogus Christian relics on the eve of Good Friday provokes a hysterical girl to demand the production of one relic in particular, and the poet comments:

> Poor soul! Why do you cry out like this for the crucified god's parts?
>   Cry for Priapus! That god's parts are the medicine you need.

In both texts, the ancient idol has been raised as the heathen counterpart to the crucifix. We may recall here that Goethe's personal reaction to crucifixes and to the Christian cross in general appears to have been one of intense, if not indeed neurotic, hatred, comparable to his equally visceral antagonism to Newton's theory of colours.

Whatever the secret implications of stanza XVII, the effects of this extraordinary flashback to the wild sexuality of youth are felt immediately. Mysteriously, the potency of the insomniac traveller is restored. The act of remembering is revealed to have the power to re-member in the physical sense as well. Yet the would-be lover does not wake his companion as we might have expected. Instead, in a surprising gesture of renunciation, he gets out of bed and resumes the other activity he was incapable of performing earlier: that of writing in his diary. The writer's powers, both sexual and creative, have been recovered. We should not simplify what the poem tells us of the reason for this new-found strength. It lies not merely in the fact that his thoughts turn again to his wife as such. Rather, it is the profoundly erotic recollection of his youthful passion for the woman who is now his wife. His bond with her evidently was and still is both erotic and personal, something much more complex and profound than the casual attraction to the pretty stranger. In Freudian terms we might say that the diarist's relationship to his wife is genital rather than phallic. It is this relationship that has acted as a 'magic love-knot' of the kind to which (l. 116) he ruefully refers.

Once again the comparison with *Elective Affinities* is illuminating. The novel's central event occurs when Eduard and Charlotte, the husband and wife, have intercourse with each other—and not really with each other: he, in his imagination, is with his beloved Ottilie, and she with her would-be lover the Captain. But on this very occasion Eduard begets, and Charlotte conceives, a child— a son whose mysterious resemblance to his 'imagined' parents betrays the 'imagined' adultery committed by his biological parents in their hearts. In *The Diary*, on the other hand, the travelling husband's libido is strongly fixated on his absent wife and thus makes him at first unable to perform the intended seduction, and later disinclined to do so. His potency is restored, but the adultery does not happen. In the novel the absent beloved inwardly replaces the wife: in the poem the absent wife inwardly supplants her rival.

All this needs to be borne in mind if we are to understand ad-equately the ambiguities of the poem's concluding lines. By having the protagonist forgo intercourse and resume his writing, Goethe has subverted the conventions of the *novella galante*. And now stanza XXIV, to the reader's even greater surprise, appears to offer a moral of deceptive simplicity: love, we are told, is a more powerful force for good than duty. But to read this statement in the obvious, banal sense, as an edifying truism, would scarcely do it justice as the conclusion of so daring and elaborate a text. The concluding lines lose their apparent simplicity as soon as we recognize that the two key words 'Pflicht' and 'Liebe' have a contextually more compelling significance here than would appear at first sight.

So far as 'Pflicht' is concerned, the context strongly suggests that in *The Diary* Goethe was using the word in its older, now extinct sense of specifically *marital* duty—as he does, for example, in *Elective Affinities*, *Torquato Tasso*, and the ballad 'The God and the Dancing-Girl'. (A comparable usage is the English cognate 'plight' in its older sense of 'promise', as in 'to plight one's troth'.) And looking beyond the context of Goethe's work we begin to realize that 'Pflicht' had been a key technical term in the legal and religious discourse on sexuality. We may safely assume that Goethe, himself a lawyer, would have been conscious of these implications. As Jean-

Louis Flandrin has reminded us, duty in the sense of 'debt' (*debitum*) had been a central notion in theological teaching on marriage and sex ever since St Paul and St Jerome.[46] Essentially, the concept of 'duty' served to regulate marital sex. Recognizing the existence of desire, the medieval Church Fathers placed husband and wife under the obligation—the 'duty'—to satisfy each other's physical needs. At the same time, lust (*voluptas*) as an end in itself was forbidden and penalized since, as St Jerome argued, 'nothing is so vile as to love one's wife as if she were a mistress'.[47]

Read in the light of this tradition, which around 1800 was still the dominant one, *The Diary* takes on a different, subtly subversive meaning. If 'Pflicht' is specifically the formal marital bond, the 'duty' to be not only faithful to one's wife but potent with her and indeed to procreate, and if 'Liebe' is not merely the conventional conjugal affection but specifically the elemental sexual desire, the libido—then Goethe's lines cannot be read as an endorsement of the centuries-old Christian teaching which, in fact, proscribed such desire. Nor can the poem be construed as an emphatic encomium of marital love or as a condemnation of extramarital love. Rather, it challenges us to a more profound reflection on the nature and the workings of desire. It distinguishes two sources of strength on which, when we 'stumble' in life (l. 190), we can rely: one is our commitment to the formal bond of marriage, but the other—love grounded in Eros—is a force more effective and reliable. Nature, under certain conditions, will prevail over culture, and triumph over it, as *Elective Affinities* demonstrates. *The Diary*, by rejecting the dominant hierarchy of values which exalts 'duty' over 'love', makes the same general point from a different perspective. As the *Roman Elegies* had done, *The Diary* affirms the very thing that Christianity has sought to contain and to regulate: the elemental, natural force of Eros.

Yet at the same time, and ironically, *The Diary* seems to suggest that while Eros is the driving force of extramarital love, it can also provide the most reliable basis for marriage. We shall be prevented from 'stumbling' into infidelity not so much by a rational sense of

[46] J.-L. Flandrin, *Le Sexe et l'Occident* (Seuil, 1981).
[47] Cf. Flandrin, 'Sex in Married Life in the Early Middle Ages', in P. Ariès and A. Béjin (eds.), *Western Sexuality*, tr. A. Forster (Blackwell, 1985).

moral obligation but by the mysterious psychosomatic workings of Eros itself. Again we may recall the parallel but contrasting situation in *Elective Affinities*: Eduard commits adultery on the level of fantasy, while on the literal level performing his conjugal duty; the diarist is about to commit adultery literally, but discovers that he could not do so without, in his fantasy, activating the erotic energies fuelled by his marriage. In neither case does an act of adultery actually occur, but in both cases the implied affirmation of marriage is couched in ambiguity and irony—a tragic irony in the novel, a conciliatory irony in the poem. There is ample justification, then, for characterizing *The Diary* as 'moral in tendency'. Eckermann was no doubt prompted to this remark by Goethe himself, who in the notes for his own *Annals* for the year 1810 had already described his new poem, in a striking phrase that resists translation, as 'erotisch-moralisch'.[48] Goethe well knew that his 'erotic morality' was ahead of his time. It foreshadows a similar posture in his great twentieth-century admirer Thomas Mann, whose *Death in Venice* is a paradigm of ironic erotic morality, as Mann himself insisted.[49]

But notwithstanding the very modern ambiguities of Goethe's text, the conception of love celebrated in *The Diary* underscores once more the close kinship of this poem to the *Roman Elegies*. There, the force of Eros was celebrated in the figure of Priapus; here, the same force is represented by the 'Iste' of stanza XVII. What this seems to suggest is a strong underlying continuity of purpose. And we may conclude that the poem of 1810 can be traced back to the same project, the same motive that had inspired the *Elegies* and provided even the more loosely organized *Venetian Epigrams* with some focus: the intention to recover for Priapus his rightful place among the deities of the day and to reclaim his central place in poetry.

[48] WA xxxvi. 399.
[49] See Mann's letter to C. M. Weber, 4 July 1920, in *Letters of Thomas Mann 1889–1955*, tr. R. and C. Winston (Secker & Warburg, 1970), 102 ff. Not surprisingly in view of the prominence of problematic sexual themes in his work, Mann was particularly interested in *The Diary*, which he seems to have first read in 1920. Echoes of it are clearly traceable in *The Magic Mountain*, *Joseph and his Brothers*, and *Doctor Faustus*. The poem plays a significant part in his fictional portrait of Goethe, *Lotte in Weimar*, in which (using Goethe's own phrase) he alludes to its 'erotic morality'. For further discussion of these connections see Vaget, *Goethe*, 140 ff.

In historical perspective, *The Diary* may be seen as documenting a fundamental and lasting reorientation in the conception of ideal marriage. Though apparently concerned with the problem of adultery, Goethe's poem actually suggests a redefinition of marriage in which Eros is viewed as a moral force and as a more powerful and reliable foundation than the dictates and restrictions of 'duty'. Compared with *Elective Affinities*, which focuses on the moral dilemma of a declining social order, namely that of the landed gentry, *The Diary* opens up a more forward-looking perspective. It invokes specifically modern, bourgeois notions which in Germany had first been proposed by the young Romantics, notably by Friedrich Schlegel in his notoriously libertinistic novel *Lucinde* (1799). So far as England is concerned, a similar development was observed by Lawrence Stone in his magisterial study *The Family, Sex and Marriage in England, 1500–1800*. According to Stone, a 'new ideal' of sexual ethics was gaining ascendency towards the end of the eighteenth century—an ideal which Stone defines as 'fusion of marriage and sexual passion'. At its innermost core, Goethe's poem argues for precisely such a 'union of wife and mistress role'.[50]

Above all, however, *The Diary* stands out as a landmark in modern erotic poetry. It ventures, thematically speaking, into quite new territory: the psychology of sexual failure. It is interesting to note that in 1907 it was discussed by Freud and his colleagues at a meeting of the Vienna Psychoanalytical Society, when Maximilian Steiner read a paper 'On Functional Impotence'. Although not identified by title, the poem referred to by both Steiner and Freud is without a doubt *The Diary*; they may have read it in a scholarly reprint which had appeared in 1904.[51] Both cite 'the poem by Goethe' as illustration of a case of 'psychic impotence'. Freud differs from Steiner in his interpretation of the psychological causes of the sexual failure in *The Diary*. Sketching a typology of impotence, he identifies as the most interesting cases 'from a psychological point of view' those 'individuals whose sexual activity cannot dispense with the psychic component; whose phantasy life predominates; or, more generally, individuals whose sexual activity is of the feminine

[50] See L. Stone, *The Family, Sex and Marriage in England, 1500–1800* (Harper & Row, 1977), 527 ff., 543 ff.

[51] Goethe, *Das Tagebuch (1810), vier unterdrückte Römische Elegien, Nicolai auf Werthers Grab*, ed. Max Mendheim (Weigel, 1904).

type. All of us civilized people (Kulturmenschen)', Freud observes, 'have some tendencies to psychic impotence.' On the basis of this general definition, Freud disagrees with Steiner, who viewed this as an example of how impotence can occur 'when one approaches a woman [. . .] with too deep respect'. Freud, by contrast, attributes the impotence to the fact that 'the libido is not available because it is bound to unconscious (repressed) ideas' or to another person, and specifically because of a 'fixation on the absent beloved'.[52] Freud, rather interestingly, refers here to the absent 'Geliebte', which means 'beloved' in a general sense, and 'mistress' in the specific sense. His remark thus goes some way towards confirming the reading of *The Diary* outlined above.

Among poets, Goethe seems to have been the first to treat the subject of impotence seriously and without prudishness. More important, *The Diary* participates fully in the decisive turn of European Romantic poetry to poetic self-consciousness. By reflecting on the interdependence of the love act and the act of writing, it illuminates the condition of the modern poet in a post-Priapean, no longer naïve age. Furthermore, this poem succeeds where much so-called erotic writing disappoints: it is light-hearted but not affected, serious but not ponderous, and it is truly daring instead of being merely frivolous. Miraculously, Goethe kept his poem free of that philosophical and religious ballast with which the German Romantics— Friedrich Schlegel, for example, but also Novalis and Brentano—so burdened the literary treatment of sexuality. On the whole, Goethe also remained immune to the fascination of the power-games of sex, that obsession which drove his contemporary, the Marquis de Sade, to ever new explorations of the recesses of the human body and mind. However, like most erotic poetry written by men, Goethe's narrative contains more than a trace of phallocentric narcissism, though this is balanced and mitigated by the element of tenderness and delicacy in the narrator's treatment of the girl (ll. 111 f., 167 f.). *The Diary* is in fact a complex and profound human document of great sophistication—qualities which combine with the elegant virtuosity of its language to make it one of the most remarkable of all Goethe's poems.

---

[52] *Minutes of the Vienna Psychoanalytic Society*, i: *1906–8* (International Universities Press, 1962), 212 ff.

SELECT BIBLIOGRAPHY

1. *German editions of Goethe's poems*

Goethes Neue Schriften, 7 vols. (Unger, Berlin, 1792–1800). Poems in vol. vii (1800). (N)

Goethes Werke: Vollständige Ausgabe letzter Hand [Complete final edition], 40 vols. (Cotta, Stuttgart, 1827–30). Poems in vols. i–iv (1827). (ALH)

Goethes Werke, herausgegeben im Auftrage der Großherzogin Sophie von Sachsen [Goethe's works, published by authority of the Grand Duchess Sophia of Saxony]. Historical-critical edition based on the ALH, with textual variants. Section I: literary works, 55 vols. (Weimar, 1887–1918). Poems in vols. i–v and liii. (Weimarer Ausgabe, WA)

Goethes Gedichte, 3 vols., ed. Emil Staiger, with commentary (Manesse Verlag, Zürich, 1949), i: *Römische Elegien* (pp. 201–42), *Venezianische Epigramme* (pp. 305–52).

Goethes Sämtliche Werke, Briefe, Tagebücher und Gespräche [Complete works, letters, diaries, and conversations], 40 vols. (Deutscher Klassiker Verlag, Frankfurt, 1987–). Poems in section I, vols. i (1987) and ii (1988), ed. Karl Eibl (i: *Römische Elegien* and *Venezianische Epigramme*, pp. 392–478), with commentary, parallel texts, and variants. (Frankfurter Ausgabe, FA)

Goethes Sämtliche Werke nach Epochen seines Schaffens [Complete works arranged by periods] (Carl Hanser Verlag, Munich, 1985–), iii/ii: *Italien und Weimar 1786–1790*, ed. Hans J. Becker *et al.* (1990); ix: *Epoche der Wahlverwandtschaften 1807–1814*, ed. Christoph Siegrist *et al.* (1987). (Münchner Ausgabe, MA)

Römische Elegien, ed. Albert Leitzmann (transcript of MS H50 only (20 elegies) with textual variants and an appendix of contemporary critical reactions) (Marcus & Webers Verlag, Bonn, 1912).

Römische Elegien (facsimile of MS H50), ed. Max Hecker, with commentary. (Insel, Leipzig, 1920).

Goethes 'Römische Elegien', ed. and introd. Dominik Jost, with commentary and textual variants (transcript of MSS H50 and H51 (24 elegies) with ALH text in parallel) (Deutsche Klassik: Verlag Dokumentation, Pullach bei München, 1974; 2nd edn. 1978).

Römische Elegien (facsimile of MS H50), ed. Hans-Georg Dewitz, postscript by Horst Rüdiger (Insel [Insel-Bücherei No. 1010], Frankfurt 1980).

2. *English translations of Goethe's poems*

Selected Verse, German text with prose tr. and introd. David Luke (Penguin, London, 1964; 2nd edn. 1972; 3rd edn. 1981; Penguin Classics 1985).

Roman Elegies and *Venetian Epigrams*, tr. and introd. Lewis Robert Lind, bilingual edn. with commentary (Kansas University Press, Lawrence, 1974).

Roman Elegies, tr. and introd. David Luke, bilingual edn. with commentary (Chatto & Windus, London, 1977).

Roman Elegies (Erotica Romana), ed. and tr. Harry Haile, as 'Goethe, Erotica Romana', *Boston University Journal*, 27 (1979), 3–19.

Selected Poems, German texts with verse tr. Michael Hamburger, Christopher Middleton, David Luke, *et al.*, Goethe's Collected Works, Suhrkamp edn., vol. i (Calder, London, 1983).

Poems and Epigrams, verse tr. Michael Hamburger (Anvil Press, London, 1983).

Roman Elegies and *The Diary*, bilingual edn. with commentary, elegiac and *ottava rima* verse tr. David Luke, introd. H. R. Vaget (Libris, London, 1988).

3. *Studies in English of Goethe's poetry and Goethe in general*

Bernhardt, Eva Dessau, *Goethe's Römische Elegien: The Poet and the Lover*, Germanic Studies in America 59 (Peter Lang, Bern, 1990).

Boyle, Nicholas, *Goethe: The Poet and the Age*, i: *The Poetry of Desire (1749–1790)* (Clarendon Press, Oxford, 1991).

Dieckmann, Liselotte, *Johann Wolfgang Goethe* (Twayne Publishers, New York, 1974).

Eissler, Kurt R., *Goethe: A Psychoanalytic Study, 1775–86* (Wayne State University Press, Detroit, 1963).

Fairley, Barker, *Goethe as Revealed in his Poetry* (Frederick Ungar, New York, 1932; repr. 1963).

——*A Study of Goethe* (Clarendon Press, Oxford, 1947).

Friedenthal, Richard, *Goethe: His Life and Times* (Weidenfeld & Nicolson, London, and The World Publishing Co., Cleveland, 1965).

Glockhamer, Heidi, 'Fama and Amor: The Function of Eroticism in Goethe's "Roman Elegies"', *Eighteenth Century Studies*, 19 (1985–6), 235–53.

Goethe Yearbook (Publications of the Goethe Society of North America), ed. Thomas P. Saine (Camden House, Columbia, SC, 1982–) (publishes articles and reviews on all aspects of Goethe and the 'Goethezeit').

Graham, Ilse, *Goethe: Portrait of the Artist* (de Gruyter, Berlin, 1977).

Haile, Harry G., *Artist in Chrysalis: A Biographical Study of Goethe in Italy* (University of Illinois Press, Urbana, 1973).

Hexter, Ralph, 'Poetic Reclamation and Goethe's "Venezianische Epigramme"', *Modern Languages Notes*, 96 (1981), 526–55.

Lee, Meredith, *Studies in Goethe's Lyric Cycles* (University of North Carolina Press, Chapel Hill, 1978).

Lewes, G. H., *The Life and Works of Goethe* (London, 1855; repr. Everyman's Library, London, 1949).

Littlejohns, Richard, 'Poetry as Autobiography: The Example of Goethe's "Römische Elegien"', *Modern Languages*, 67 (1986), 149–54.

Lukacs, Georg, *Goethe and his Age* (essays) (Merlin Press, London, 1968).

Publications of the English Goethe Society, 1–12 (1886–1912) and NS 1– (1924–) (these contain articles on numerous aspects of Goethe; an index has also been provided by A. C. Weaver (*Index to the P.E.G.S. 1886–1970*, Leeds, 1973)).

Reed, T. J., 'The *Goethezeit* and its Aftermath', in J. M. S. Pasley (ed.), *Germany: A Companion to German Studies* (Methuen, London, 1972), 493–553.

———*The Classical Centre: Goethe and Weimar 1775–1832* (Croom Helm, London, and Barnes & Noble, New York, 1980; Oxford University Press, Oxford, 1986).

——— *Goethe*, Past Masters Series (Oxford University Press, Oxford, 1984).

Trevelyan, Humphrey, *Goethe and the Greeks* (Cambridge University Press, Cambridge, 1941; repr. 1981 with foreword by H. Lloyd-Jones).

Wilkinson, E. M., and Willoughby, L. A., *Goethe: Poet and Thinker* (essays) (Edward Arnold, London, 1962).

——— 'Sexual Attitudes in Goethe's Life and Works', in E. M. Wilkinson (ed.), *Goethe Revisited* (Calder, London, and Riverrun Press, New York, 1984), 170–84.

Ziolkowski, Theodore, *The Classical German Elegy, 1795–1950* (Princeton University Press, Princeton, 1980), 55–88.

CHRONOLOGY

1749   (28 Aug.) Johann Wolfgang Goethe born in Frankfurt am Main to well-to-do middle-class parents (Johann Caspar Goethe (1710–82) and Catharina Elisabeth, née Textor (1731–1808)).

c.1770–5   Goethe's youthful 'Sturm und Drang' period, during which he becomes famous as a lyric poet and as the author of *Götz von Berlichingen* and *The Sorrows of Young Werther*; an early version of *Faust* ('Urfaust') is also written but not published.

1775   (April–July) Engagement to Lili Schönemann (1758–1817).
Goethe settles in Weimar at the invitation of the reigning Duke Karl August (1757–1828), who becomes his close friend.

1775–86   Goethe's first Weimar years (various ministerial duties, responsibility for theatrical productions, growing interest in the natural sciences, *amitié amoureuse* with a married lady, Charlotte von Stein). Ennoblement (1782) as 'von Goethe' by the Emperor Joseph II at Karl August's request.

1786 (Sept.)–1788 (June)   Goethe's first visit to Italy (the 'Italian Journey'); from Nov. 1786 until Apr. 1788 chiefly in Rome. Completion of *Iphigenia in Tauris*, continuation of *Torquato Tasso* and *Faust*.

1788   (Feb.) Liaison in Rome with a young widow, ?'Faustina' Antonini. (June) Goethe returns to Weimar. Breach with Charlotte von Stein. (July) Goethe meets Christiane Vulpius (1765–1816) and begins living with her.
(Oct.) Goethe begins writing the *Roman Elegies* (originally planned as *Erotica Romana*). Studies Catullus, Propertius, and other models including the *Carmina Priapea*.

1789–90   Completion of *Torquato Tasso* and the *Roman Elegies*; publication of the first collected edition of Goethe's works. His son August born (Dec. 1789). *Roman Elegies* withheld from publication.

1790   Second Italian journey, to meet Dowager Duchess Anna Amalia and escort her home. In Venice 31 Mar. to 22 May; *Venetian Epigrams* written at this time. Publication of the *Faust* 'Fragment'.

1794   Beginning of Goethe's friendship and intellectual partnership with Friedrich Schiller (1759–1805).

1795   (June) Publication of the *Roman Elegies* ('Elegien: Rom 1788') in Schiller's new literary periodical *Die Horen* (I, III, XVII, and XXIV still withheld).

(Dec.) Publication of an edited selection of 103 *Venetian Epigrams* in Schiller's *Musenalmanach* for the year 1796. In Vienna the periodical is banned by the censors.

1796   Completion of the novel *Wilhelm Meister's Apprenticeship*, the origins of which date back to 1777.

1797   Completion and publication of the epic idyll *Hermann and Dorothea*; resumption of work on *Faust* under Schiller's influence.

1800   104 *Venetian Epigrams* (dedicated to Anna Amalia) published in the second collected edition of Goethe's works; this remains the official 'cycle' in subsequent editions, many others being withheld.

1805   (9 May) Death of Schiller.

1806   (19 Oct.) Marriage to Christiane Vulpius formalized.

1808   Publication of *Faust Part One*.
       (Oct.) Goethe meets Napoleon Bonaparte at Erfurt.

1808-9   Work on the novel *Elective Affinities* (published 1809); probable conception of *The Diary* at this time.

1810   (Apr.) Goethe finishes *The Diary*; he regards it as unpublishable, but shows it or reads it aloud to friends from time to time.

1814-16   Goethe writes the *Westöstlicher Divan*, a collection of poems inspired by the medieval Persian poetry of Hafiz and by his love for a married lady, Marianne von Willemer (1784-1860).

1816   (6 June) Death of Christiane.

1823   Goethe meets Ulrike von Levetzow (1804-99) at Marienbad, and through the intermediacy of Karl August makes a proposal of marriage to her, which is declined. Writes the 'Marienbad Elegy', the centre-piece of a group of poems called 'Trilogy of Passion'.

1823-32   Johann Peter Eckermann's conversations with Goethe (published after Goethe's death).

1825-31   Completion and partial publication of *Faust Part Two*, as part of Goethe's final edition of his works (*Ausgabe letzter Hand*).

1828   (14 June) Death of Grand Duke Karl August.

1830   (26 Oct.) Death of Goethe's son August.

1832   (22 Mar.) Death of Goethe. Posthumous complete publication of *Faust Part Two*.

1861   First pirated publication of *The Diary* by Salomon Hirzel, who claimed to have seen Goethe's lost autograph MS or a copy of it.

1879-80   Further pirated editions; copies seized by police in Vienna and Koblenz.

1887–1919   Publication of the official historical-critical 'Weimar' edition of Goethe's works under the patronage of the Grand Duchess Sophia.

1910   *The Diary* printed in a supplementary volume of the Weimar edition, with most of line 135 omitted.

1910, 1914   Remaining unpublished *Venetian Epigrams* material released by the Goethe archive.

1914   The Weimar edition prints the missing words of *The Diary* inconspicuously among textual variants in a further supplementary volume.

RÖMISCHE ELEGIEN

ROMAN ELEGIES

I
[PROLOG]

Hier ist mein Garten bestellt, hier wart ich die Blumen der Liebe,
    Wie sie die Muse gewählt, weislich in Beete verteilt.
Früchte bringenden Zweig, die goldenen Früchte des Lebens,
    Glücklich pflanzt ich sie an, warte mit Freuden sie nun.
Stehe du hier an der Seite, Priap! ich habe von Dieben
    Nichts zu befürchten, und frei pflück und genieße wer mag.
Nur bemerke die Heuchler, entnervte, verschämte Verbrecher;
    Nahet sich einer und blinzt über den zierlichen Raum,
Ekelt an Früchten der reinen Natur, so straf ihn von hinten
    Mit dem Pfahle, der dir rot von den Hüften entspringt.   10

I*
[PROLOGUE]

Here my garden is growing, the flowers of Eros* I tend here;
    They are the Muse's own choice, bedded out wisely they bloom.
Branches that bear ripe fruit, the golden fruit of the life-tree:
    Gladly I planted them once, gladly I nurture them now.
Stand here beside them, Priapus! I've nothing to fear from
      marauders;
    Anyone's welcome, it's all free to be picked and enjoyed.
But keep the hypocrites out, those miscreants flaccid and
      shamefaced!
    If one should dare to approach, peep at our charming domain,
Turn up his nose at the fruits of pure Nature, just punish his
      backside
    With one thrust of that red stake-shaft that sprouts from your
      loins.   10

II

Saget, Steine, mir an, o sprecht, ihr hohen Paläste!
  Straßen, redet ein Wort! Genius, regst du dich nicht?
Ja, es ist alles beseelt in deinen heiligen Mauern,
  Ewige Roma; nur mir schweiget noch alles so still.
O wer flüstert mir zu, an welchem Fenster erblick ich
  Einst das holde Geschöpf, das mich versengend erquickt?
Ahn ich die Wege noch nicht, durch die ich immer und immer,
  Zu ihr und von ihr zu gehn, opfre die köstliche Zeit?
Noch betracht ich Kirch und Palast, Ruinen und Säulen,
  Wie ein bedächtiger Mann schicklich die Reise benutzt.   20
Doch bald ist es vorbei; dann wird ein einziger Tempel,
  Amors Tempel, nur sein, der den Geweihten empfängt.
Eine Welt zwar bist du, o Rom; doch ohne die Liebe
  Wäre die Welt nicht die Welt, wäre denn Rom auch nicht Rom.

II

Speak to me, stones, oh say, you lofty palaces, tell me—
    Streets, are you lost for a word? Genius, how idly you sleep!*
Yes—though within your sacred walls, oh perennial city,
    All is alive and astir, still all is silent for me.
Who shall whisper the secret, and where one day at a window
    Shall I first see her, when first burn with love's life-giving fire?
Oh, those well-trodden paths that will lead me to her and from her,
    Squandering my hours away—can I not guess at them yet?
Still I am gazing at churches and palaces, ruins and columns,
    Carefully seeing the sights, as a good traveller should.   20
But all this will be over soon, and the city a temple—
    Love's great temple, and I'll be its initiate then.
Rome, though you are a whole world, yet a world without love
        would be no world,
    And if there were no love, Rome would not even be Rome.

III

Mehr als ich ahndete schön, das Glück, es ist mir geworden;
    Amor führte mich klug allen Palästen vorbei.
Ihm ist es lange bekannt, auch hab ich es selbst wohl erfahren,
    Was ein goldnes Gemach hinter Tapeten verbirgt.
Nennet blind ihn und Knaben und ungezogen, ich kenne,
    Kluger Amor, dich wohl, nimmer bestechlicher Gott!   30
Uns verführten sie nicht, die majestätschen Fassaden,
    Nicht der galante Balkon, weder das ernste Kortil.
Eilig ging es vorbei, und niedre zierliche Pforte
    Nahm den Führer zugleich, nahm den Verlangenden auf.
Alles verschafft er mir da, hilft alles und alles erhalten,
    Streuet jeglichen Tag frischere Rosen mir auf.
Hab ich den Himmel nicht hier? — Was gibst du, schöne Borghese,
    Nipotina, was gibst deinen Geliebten du mehr?
Tafel, Gesellschaft und Kors' und Spiel und Oper und Bälle,
    Amorn rauben sie nur oft die gelegenste Zeit.   40
Ekel bleibt mir Gezier und Putz, und hebet am Ende
    Sich ein brokatener Rock nicht wie ein wollener auf?
Oder will sie bequem den Freund im Busen verbergen,
    Wünscht er von alle dem Schmuck nicht schon behend sie
        befreit?
Müssen nicht jene Juwelen und Spitzen, Polster und Fischbein
    Alle zusammen herab, eh er die Liebliche fühlt?
Näher haben wir das! Schon fällt dein wollenes Kleidchen,
    So wie der Freund es gelöst, faltig zum Boden hinab.
Eilig trägt er das Kind, in leichter linnener Hülle,
    Wie es der Amme geziemt, scherzend aufs Lager hinan.   50
Ohne das seidne Gehäng und ohne gestickte Matratzen,
    Stehet es, zweien bequem, frei in dem weiten Gemach.
Nehme dann Jupiter mehr von seiner Juno, es lasse
    Wohler sich, wenn er es kann, irgend ein Sterblicher sein.
Uns ergötzen die Freuden des echten nacketen Amors
    Und des geschaukelten Betts lieblicher knarrender Ton.

III

More than I ever had hoped, what happiness I have been granted!
    Love led me wisely through Rome, passing its palaces by.
He has long known, and I myself have learnt it the hard way,
    What the fine tapestries hide in all those bedrooms of gold.
Call Eros* blind if you like, and a boy, and wanton: I know him
    And his sagacity well, this incorruptible god.   30
Those majestic façades could not tempt us aside, nor the solemn
    Courtyards, the balconies well suited to nights of romance.
On we pressed, till at last a door both humble and charming
    Willingly welcomed the guide, welcomed the suppliant in.
Here there is nothing I lack, for he is a constant provider;
    Fresh are the roses that Love scatters each day on my path.
Is this not heaven itself? What more, fair Princess Borghese,
    Fair Nipotina,* can you give for your lovers' delight?
Dinners and parties, walks or drives down the Corso, or
    card-games,
    Operas, dances—they waste so much good love-making time!   40
I have grown sick of adornments and finery: are not, when all's
    done,
    Skirts of brocade and of wool equally easy to lift?
How can a woman embrace her lover in comfort unless she
    First, at his eager behest, sheds all her dainty array?
Will he not want those jewels and laces, that whalebone and
    quilted
    Satin discarded at once, freeing her for his caress?
We make short work of all that!—In a trice I unfasten this simple
    Woollen dress, and it drops, slips in its folds to the floor.
Quickly, cajolingly, like a good nurse, I carry my darling—
    Only a light linen shift covers her now—to the bed.   50
Here are no curtains of silk, no embroidered mattresses; freely
    In the wide bedroom it stands, ample in width to take two.
Now not Jupiter's pleasure in Juno's embraces is greater,
    And no mortal's content vies, I will wager, with mine!
Ours is the true, the authentic, the naked Love; and beneath us,
    Rocking in rhythm, the bed creaks the dear song of our joy.

IV

Ehret, wen ihr auch wollt! Nun bin ich endlich geborgen!
    Schöne Damen und ihr, Herren der feineren Welt,
Fraget nach Oheim und Vetter und alten Muhmen und Tanten,
    Und dem gebundnen Gespräch folge das traurige Spiel.   60
Auch ihr übrigen fahret mir wohl, in großen und kleinen
    Zirkeln, die ihr mich oft nah der Verzweiflung gebracht.
Wiederholet, politisch und zwecklos, jegliche Meinung,
    Die den Wandrer mit Wut über Europa verfolgt.
So verfolgte das Liedchen *Malbrough* den reisenden Briten
    Einst von Paris nach Livorn, dann von Livorno nach Rom,
Weiter nach Napel hinunter; und wär er nach Smyrna gesegelt,
    Malbrough! empfing ihn auch dort! Malbrough! im Hafen das
        Lied.
Und so mußt ich bis jetzt auf allen Tritten und Schritten
    Schelten hören das Volk, schelten der Könige Rat.   70
Nun entdeckt ihr mich nicht so bald in meinem Asyle,
    Das mir Amor der Fürst, königlich schützend, verlieh.
Hier bedecket er mich mit seinem Fittich; die Liebste
    Fürchtet, römisch gesinnt, wütende Gallier nicht;
Sie erkundigt sich nie nach neuer Märe, sie spähet
    Sorglich den Wünschen des Manns, dem sie sich eignete, nach.
Sie ergetzt sich an ihm, dem freien, rüstigen Fremden,
    Der von Bergen und Schnee, hölzernen Häusern erzählt;
Teilt die Flammen, die sie in seinem Busen entzündet,
    Freut sich, daß er das Gold nicht wie der Römer bedenkt.   80
Besser ist ihr Tisch nun bestellt; es fehlet an Kleidern,
    Fehlet am Wagen ihr nicht, der nach der Oper sie bringt.
Mutter und Tochter erfreun sich ihres nordischen Gastes,
    Und der Barbare beherrscht römischen Busen und Leib.

IV

Now at last I am home and dry! Take your flattery elsewhere,
    My fair ladies, my fine gentlemen of the *beau monde*!
Chatter politely about your old aunts and uncles and cousins,
    Then let some tedious game follow the elegant talk.   60
Goodbye all of you, social circles and gatherings, great and
    Small! How often you've half driven me out of my mind!
Travellers barely escape your political vain repetitions,
    Right across Europe one runs from their relentless pursuit.*
Thus the English were plagued by the song *Malbrouk** on their
    travels:
    Paris and Leghorn and Rome rang with it: southwards they fled,
Only to hear it in Naples; and even in far-distant Smyrna
    They would have sailed into port to a great cry of 'Malbrouk'!
So, hitherto, wherever I went, I would hear all the gossip,
    Hear them all cursing the mob, cursing the folly of kings.   70
But you'll not easily find out now the retreat I have fled to;
    For Prince Eros, my host, royally shelters me here.
Under his wings I am hidden, along with my darling; she fears no
    Gallic frenzy,* I know she's a true Roman at heart.
She has no ears for the latest political rumours; she only
    Cares for the man of her choice, watching his wishes and needs.
She is delighted by him, this free and vigorous stranger,
    And with his tales about snow, mountains, and houses of wood;
She has kindled a fire in his heart, and shares it, rejoicing
    Too in his liberal purse (men are so mean here in Rome).   80
Now she eats better than ever before, and has plenty of dresses;
    Drives to the opera now, fetched in an elegant coach.
Mother and daughter are pleased with their northern guest, and a
    Roman
    Bosom and body now lie under barbarian rule.

V

Laß dich, Geliebte, nicht reun, daß du mir so schnell dich ergeben!
   Glaub es, ich denke nicht frech, denke nicht niedrig von dir.
Vielfach wirken die Pfeile des Amor: einige ritzen,
   Und vom schleichenden Gift kranket auf Jahre das Herz.
Aber mächtig befiedert, mit frisch geschliffener Schärfe
   Dringen die andern ins Mark, zünden behende das Blut.   90
In der heroischen Zeit, da Götter und Göttinnen liebten,
   Folgte Begierde dem Blick, folgte Genuß der Begier.
Glaubst du, es habe sich lange die Göttin der Liebe besonnen,
   Als im Idäischen Hain einst ihr Anchises gefiel?
Hätte Luna gesäumt, den schönen Schläfer zu küssen,
   O, so hätt ihn geschwind, neidend, Aurora geweckt.
Hero erblickte Leandern am lauten Fest, und behende
   Stürzte der Liebende sich heiß in die nächtliche Flut.
Rhea Silvia wandelt, die fürstliche Jungfrau, der Tiber
   Wasser zu schöpfen, hinab, und sie ergreifet der Gott.   100
So erzeugte die Söhne sich Mars! — Die Zwillinge tränket
   Eine Wölfin, und Rom nennt sich die Fürstin der Welt.

V

Darling, do not regret the promptness of your surrender!
  I think no less of you now, you have not lost my respect.
Eros has arrows that work many ways: some merely will scratch us,
  And as the slow venom acts, so the heart sickens for years.
But there are others, strong-feathered and freshly pointed and
    sharpened—
  Right to the marrow they pierce, quickly they kindle the blood.   90
In the heroic age, when a god fell in love with a goddess,
  Passion was born at a glance, and was assuaged in a trice.
Do you suppose that Venus herself, when she fancied Anchises*
  In the Idaean grove, pondered for long what to do?
Did the Moon-goddess think twice when she kissed the fair
    sleeping Endymion?*
  No! for the envious Dawn soon would have waked him instead.
At the loud festival Hero set eyes on Leander:* and that same
  Night he plunged into the sea, hot with impatient desire.
Rhea Sylvia,* the royal virgin, went down to the Tiber
  Fetching water, and Mars snatched her up into his arms;   100
Thus the War-god fathered his sons. Twin brothers a she-wolf
  Suckled, the founders of Rome: Rome now is queen of the
    world.

VI

Fromm sind wir Liebende, still verehren wir alle Dämonen,
    Wünschen uns jeglichen Gott, jegliche Göttin geneigt.
Und so gleichen wir euch, o römische Sieger! Den Göttern
    Aller Völker der Welt bietet ihr Wohnungen an,
Habe sie schwarz und streng aus altem Basalt der Ägypter,
    Oder ein Grieche sie weiß, reizend, aus Marmor geformt.
Doch verdrießet es nicht die Ewigen, wenn wir besonders
    Weihrauch köstlicher Art Einer der Göttlichen streun.   110
Ja, wir bekennen euch gern: es bleiben unsre Gebete,
    Unser täglicher Dienst Einer besonders geweiht.
Schalkhaft, munter und ernst begehen wir heimliche Feste,
    Und das Schweigen geziemt allen Geweihten genau.
Eh an die Ferse lockten wir selbst durch gräßliche Taten
    Uns die Erinnyen her, wagten es eher, des Zeus
Hartes Gericht am rollenden Rad und am Felsen zu dulden,
    Als dem reizenden Dienst unser Gemüt zu entziehn.
Diese Göttin, sie heißt *Gelegenheit*; lernet sie kennen!
    Sie erscheinet euch oft, immer in andrer Gestalt.   120
Tochter des Proteus möchte sie sein, mit Thetis gezeuget,
    Deren verwandelte List manchen Heroen betrog.
So betriegt nun die Tochter den Unerfahrnen, den Blöden:
    Schlummernde necket sie stets, Wachende fliegt sie vorbei;
Gern ergibt sie sich nur dem raschen, tätigen Manne,
    Dieser findet sie zahm, spielend und zärtlich und hold.
Einst erschien sie auch mir, ein bräunliches Mädchen, die Haare
    Fielen ihr dunkel und reich über die Stirne herab,
Kurze Locken ringelten sich ums zierliche Hälschen,
    Ungeflochtenes Haar krauste vom Scheitel sich auf.   130
Und ich verkannte sie nicht, ergriff die Eilende, lieblich
    Gab sie Umarmung und Kuß bald mir gelehrig zurück.
O wie war ich beglückt! — Doch stille, die Zeit ist vorüber,
    Und umwunden bin ich, römische Flechten, von euch.

VI

Lovers are pious: we worship all supernatural beings,
  Gods and goddesses all, humbly their favour we beg.
Thus we resemble the conquering Romans, for they too would
    offer
  Homes to the whole world's gods, gods of all peoples alike,
Whether Egyptians had carved them austerely from blackest old
    basalt
  Or they'd been fashioned by Greeks, marble and gleaming and
    white.
But the Immortals will not be incensed if as lovers we scatter
  Choicest of incense to one goddess we chiefly revere.   110
For we must gladly confess there is one whom we supplicate
    daily—
  Homage to one above all others we ardently pay.
Roguish and merry and grave are the rites of our secret observance,
  And a strict silence we keep, as all initiates must.
Rather by horrible deeds we ourselves would call up the Furies
  Hot on our heels, or risk Jupiter's sentence of doom
And endure to be whirled on a wheel or chained to a cliff-face,*
  Than be unmindful of this service that holds us in thrall.
Our dear goddess is called *Opportunity*: do you not know her?
  Often she comes to you, each time in a different guise.   120
She is the daughter of Proteus, perhaps, engendered with Thetis,*
  Whose self-altering skill baffled the heroes of old.
Thus now their daughter deceives the inexperienced, the dullard,
  Flirting with any who nap, fleeting past all who keep watch.
Only to active resolute spirits she gladly surrenders:
  With such a man she is tame, playful and tender and kind.
Thus it was that one day she appeared to me,* as a dark-haired
  Girl: an abundance of locks tumbled down over her brow,
Shorter ringlets entwined her delicate neck, and unbraided
  Hair rose boldly in waves over the crown of her head.   130
And I knew her, I seized her as she went hurrying by me;
  Apt in response, she returned kiss and embrace with a will.
Oh, how happy I was!—But enough, that time is no longer,
  And I am captive and bound now, Roman tresses, by you.

VII

Froh empfind ich mich nun auf klassischem Boden begeistert;
   Vor- und Mitwelt spricht lauter und reizender mir.
Hier befolg ich den Rat, durchblättre die Werke der Alten
   Mit geschäftiger Hand, täglich mit neuem Genuß.
Aber die Nächte hindurch hält Amor mich anders beschäftigt;
   Werd ich auch halb nur gelehrt, bin ich doch doppelt beglückt.   140
Und belehr ich mich nicht, indem ich des lieblichen Busens
   Formen spähe, die Hand leite die Hüften hinab?
Dann versteh ich den Marmor erst recht; ich denk und vergleiche,
   Sehe mit fühlendem Aug, fühle mit sehender Hand.
Raubt die Liebste denn gleich mir einige Stunden des Tages,
   Gibt sie Stunden der Nacht mir zur Entschädigung hin.
Wird doch nicht immer geküßt, es wird vernünftig gesprochen;
   Überfällt sie der Schlaf, lieg ich und denke mir viel.
Oftmals hab ich auch schon in ihren Armen gedichtet
   Und des Hexameters Maß leise mit fingernder Hand   150
Ihr auf den Rücken gezählt. Sie atmet in lieblichem Schlummer,
   Und es durchglühet ihr Hauch mir bis ins Tiefste die Brust.
Amor schüret die Lamp indes und denket der Zeiten,
   Da er den nämlichen Dienst seinen Triumvirn getan.

VII

Now on classical soil I stand, inspired and elated:
  Past and present speak plain, charm me as never before.
Here I follow the counsels and busily thumb through the writings
  Of the ancients,* and each day with increasing delight.
But at the love-god's behest, by night my business is different;
  Half of my scholarship's lost, yet I have double the fun.   140
And is not this education, to study the shape of her lovely
  Breasts, and down over her hip slide my adventuring hand?
Marble comes doubly alive for me then, as I ponder, comparing,
  Seeing with vision that feels, feeling with fingers that see.
What if my darling deprive me of some few hours of daytime?
  Hours of night as a rich recompense she can bestow.
Though we spend some of them kissing, we spend others sensibly
    talking,
  And when she sinks into sleep, wakeful and thoughtful I lie.
Often I even compose my poetry in her embraces,
  Counting hexameter beats, tapping them out on her back   150
Softly, with one hand's fingers. She sweetly breathes in her
    slumber,
  Warmly the glow of her breath pierces the depths of my heart.
Eros recalls, as he tends our lamp, how he did the same service
  For his Triumvirs, the three poets of Love,* long ago.

VIII

'Kannst du, o Grausamer! mich in solchen Worten betrüben?
  Reden so bitter und hart liebende Männer bei euch?
Wenn das Volk mich verklagt, ich muß es dulden! und bin ich
  Etwa nicht schuldig? Doch ach! schuldig nur bin ich mit dir!
Diese Kleider, sie sind der neidischen Nachbarin Zeugen,
  Daß die Witwe nicht mehr einsam den Gatten beweint.   160
Bist du ohne Bedacht nicht oft bei Mondschein gekommen,
  Grau, im dunkeln Surtout, hinten gerundet das Haar?
Hast du dir scherzend nicht selbst die geistliche Maske gewählet?
  Solls ein Prälate denn sein! gut, der Prälate bist du.
In dem geistlichen Rom, kaum scheint es zu glauben, doch schwör
    ich:
  Nie hat ein Geistlicher sich meiner Umarmung gefreut.
Arm war ich leider! und jung, und wohlbekannt den Verführern;
  Falconieri hat mir oft in die Augen gegafft,
Und ein Kuppler Albanis mich, mit gewichtigen Zetteln,
  Bald nach Ostia, bald nach den vier Brunnen gelockt.   170
Aber wer nicht kam, war das Mädchen. So hab ich von Herzen
  Rotstrumpf immer gehaßt und Violettstrumpf dazu.
Denn "ihr Mädchen bleibt am Ende doch die Betrognen",
  Sagte der Vater, wenn auch leichter die Mutter es nahm.
Und so bin ich denn auch am Ende betrogen! Du zürnest
  Nur zum Scheine mit mir, weil du zu fliehen gedenkst.
Geh! Ihr seid der Frauen nicht wert! Wir tragen die Kinder
  Unter dem Herzen, und so tragen die Treue wir auch;

VIII

'How can you hurt me by saying such things? Are lovers so cruel?
　　Do all you men from the north talk in this hard, bitter way?
Public blame I must bear without complaining, for that I'm
　　Guilty how can I deny?—but it is only with you!
These fine clothes are proof to my envious neighbour, she knows
　　now
　　　　That I'm no longer alone, mourning the husband I lost.* 160
Have you not often enough come here, unthinking, by moonlight,
　　Grey, in a long dark coat, hair done in clerical style,
Not in a pigtail? You chose the disguise, you practical joker!
　　So it's a prelate I love? Yes—you're my prelate, who else?
In this priest-ridden city—believe it or not, but I'll swear it—
　　Who has had favours from me? Never a priest in all Rome!
Yes, I was poor, and young, and well known to seducers; and often
　　Falconieri would cast eyes on me, often some pimp
Of Albani's* would try to entice me to Quattro Fontane
　　Or to Ostia—they'd bring messages heavy with coin; 170
But did I go? Not I! For in fact those clerical gaiters
　　Always gave me the creeps, scarlet and purple* alike.
For as my father would say (though my mother would look on the
　　bright side):
　　　　"It's you girls, after all, who are the dupes in the end!"
And so it proves; in the end you too have deceived me. Your
　　anger's
　　　　Only a pretext, a sham; you want to leave me, I know.
Go, then! You men are not worthy of women; we carry your
　　children
　　　　Under our hearts, and it's there, there we bear faith to you too.

Aber ihr Männer, ihr schüttet mit eurer Kraft und Begierde
  Auch die Liebe zugleich in den Umarmungen aus!'   180
Also sprach die Geliebte und nahm den Kleinen vom Stuhle,
  Drückt' ihn küssend ans Herz, Tränen entquollen dem Blick.
Und wie saß ich beschämt, daß Reden feindlicher Menschen
  Dieses liebliche Bild mir zu beflecken vermocht!
Dunkel brennt das Feuer nur augenblicklich und dampfet,
  Wenn das Wasser die Glut stürzend und jählings verhüllt;
Aber sie reinigt sich schnell, verjagt die trübenden Dämpfe,
  Neuer und mächtiger dringt leuchtende Flamme hinauf.

But you menfolk, when you embrace us you spill all your strength
    out,
    All your desire out at once—and your love goes the same way.'   180
Thus my darling reproached me, with tears in her eyes, and she
    lifted
    Her little boy* from his chair, kissing him, hugging him tight.
There I sat, so ashamed to have let such malice and slander
    Poison my mind with mistrust, spoiling an image so dear.
Fire burns smoky and dark when a sudden deluge of water
    Dashes its ardour, but soon blazes up brightly again;
In a mere moment it clears, driving off the vapours that dulled
    it—
    Then with what vigour, what fresh brilliance its flames are
    revived!

IX

O wie fühl ich in Rom mich so froh! gedenk ich der Zeiten,
    Da mich ein graulicher Tag hinten im Norden umfing,   190
Trübe der Himmel und schwer auf meine Scheitel sich senkte,
    Farb- und gestaltlos die Welt um den Ermatteten lag,
Und ich über mein Ich, des unbefriedigten Geistes
    Düstre Wege zu spähn, still in Betrachtung versank.
Nun umleuchtet der Glanz des helleren Äthers die Stirne;
    Phöbus rufet, der Gott, Formen und Farben hervor.
Sternhell glänzet die Nacht, sie klingt von weichen Gesängen,
    Und mir leuchtet der Mond heller als nordischer Tag.
Welche Seligkeit ward mir Sterblichem! Träum ich? Empfänget
    Dein ambrosisches Haus, Jupiter Vater, den Gast?   200
Ach! hier lieg ich und strecke nach deinen Knieen die Hände
    Flehend aus. O vernimm, Jupiter Xenius, mich!
Wie ich hereingekommen, ich kanns nicht sagen: es faßte
    Hebe den Wandrer und zog mich in die Hallen heran.
Hast du ihr einen Heroen herauf zu führen geboten?
    Irrte die Schöne? Vergib! Laß mir des Irrtums Gewinn!
Deine Tochter Fortuna, sie auch! Die herrlichsten Gaben
    Teilt als ein Mädchen sie aus, wie es die Laune gebeut.
Bist du der wirtliche Gott? O dann so verstoße den Gastfreund
    Nicht von deinem Olymp wieder zur Erde hinab!   210
'Dichter! wohin versteigest du dich?' — Vergib mir; der hohe
    Kapitolinische Berg ist dir ein zweiter Olymp.
Dulde mich, Jupiter, hier, und Hermes führe mich später,
    Cestius' Mal vorbei, leise zum Orkus hinab.

IX

Oh, how happy I feel here in Rome, when I think of the old
    days—
  Dull grey days, till I fled from the imprisoning north!   190
Leaden lugubrious skies weighed down on me, bowing my spirits:
  Colour and shape there was none in that whole wearisome
    world.*
There, wrapped up in myself, I explored in silent moroseness
  Gloomy and shadowy paths of my unsatisfied mind.
Now in this shining ether a brighter radiance surrounds me:
  Here, at the sun-god's behest, colours and forms have appeared.
Here the nights are brilliant with stars and full of soft music,
  And the moonlight outglows lustreless northerly day.
Can a mere mortal enjoy such bliss? Am I dreaming? Oh father
  Jupiter, am I a guest in your ambrosial halls?   200
Ah, I lie and extend my hands as a suppliant to you,
  Here at your knees: oh hear, hear me, guest-honouring Jove!*
Heaven knows how I got in—the goddess of Youth* must have
    snatched me
  Up, as I wandered on earth, into your palace on high.
Did you command her to bring some hero, and did the fair Hebe
  Make some mistake? Then let me profit from that, by your
    grace!
See, your daughter Fortuna, she too is a generous-hearted
  Girl, and how sweet are the gifts lavished on men by her
    whims!
Are you the god of Hospitality?* Do not reject me
  Then, oh Olympian host, hurling me back down to earth!   210
'Poet! what flights of fancy are these?'—Forgive me; your home
    from
  Home, the Capitoline Hill, high as Olympus it stands.
Jupiter, let me stay here! until Hermes* quietly leads me
  Down past Cestius' tomb,* down to the land of the dead.

X

Wenn du mir sagst, du habest als Kind, Geliebte, den Menschen
  Nicht gefallen, und dich habe die Mutter verschmäht,
Bis du größer geworden und still dich entwickelt, ich glaub es:
  Gerne denk ich mir dich als ein besonderes Kind.
Fehlet Bildung und Farbe doch auch der Blüte des Weinstocks,
  Wenn die Beere, gereift, Menschen und Götter entzückt.   220

X

When you were little, my darling, you tell me nobody liked you—
  Even your mother, you say, scorned you, until as the years
Passed, you quietly grew and matured; and I can believe it—
  It's rather pleasant to think you were a strange little child.
For though the flower of a vine may be still unformed and lack
    lustre,
  In the ripe grape it yields nectar for gods and for men.   220

XI

Herbstlich leuchtet die Flamme vom ländlich geselligen Herde,
    Knistert und glänzet, wie rasch! sausend vom Reisig empor.
Diesen Abend erfreut sie mich mehr; denn eh noch zur Kohle
    Sich das Bündel verzehrt, unter die Asche sich neigt,
Kommt mein liebliches Mädchen. Dann flammen Reisig und
      Scheite,
    Und die erwärmete Nacht wird uns ein glänzendes Fest.
Morgen frühe geschäftig verläßt sie das Lager der Liebe,
    Weckt aus der Asche behend Flammen aufs neue hervor.
Denn vor andern verlieh der Schmeichlerin Amor die Gabe,
    Freude zu wecken, die kaum still wie zu Asche versank.   230

XI

Now on the rustic hearth an autumnal welcoming fire glows,
　　Kindled from crackling wood, brilliant with uprushing flame.
And tonight it delights me still more, for this bundle of twigs will
　　Still be burning, not yet crumbled to ember and ash,
When my darling arrives. The twigs and faggots will blaze up,
　　And we shall make the night warm—what a fine feast it will be!
Early tomorrow she'll busily rise from the bed of our loving;
　　Quickly the ashes she'll stir, soon the bright flame she'll renew.
For this especial gift Love gave to my dearest of charmers:
　　Pleasure no sooner burns low than she can wake it again.　　230

XII

Alexander und Cäsar und Heinrich und Friedrich, die Großen,
  Gäben die Hälfte mir gern ihres erworbenen Ruhms,
Könnt ich auf Eine Nacht dies Lager jedem vergönnen;
  Aber die armen, sie hält strenge des Orkus Gewalt.
Freue dich also, Lebendger, der lieberwärmeten Stätte,
  Ehe den fliehenden Fuß schauerlich Lethe dir netzt.

XII

Alexander and Caesar and Henry and Frederick,* those great
    kings,
  Gladly would yield up to me, each of them, half of his fame,
If by my leave he might lie in this bed even one little night long;
  But, poor souls, they are dead; Hades imprisons them all.
Therefore rejoice, living man, in the place that is warm with your
    loving:
  Cold on your shuddering foot Lethe's dread water will lap.

XIII

Euch, o Grazien, legt die wenigen Blätter ein Dichter
    Auf den reinen Altar, Knospen der Rose dazu,
Und er tut es getrost. Der Künstler freuet sich seiner
    Werkstatt, wenn sie um ihn immer ein Pantheon scheint.   240
Jupiter senket die göttliche Stirn, und Juno erhebt sie;
    Phöbus schreitet hervor, schüttelt das lockige Haupt;
Trocken schauet Minerva herab, und Hermes, der leichte,
    Wendet zur Seite den Blick, schalkisch und zärtlich zugleich.
Aber nach Bacchus, dem weichen, dem träumenden, hebet Cythere
    Blicke der süßen Begier, selbst in dem Marmor noch feucht.
Seiner Umarmung gedenket sie gern und scheinet zu fragen:
    Sollte der herrliche Sohn uns an der Seite nicht stehn?

XIII*

These few leaves are a poet's oblation, oh Graces: on your pure
    Altar he lays them, and these rosebuds he offers as well,
And he has done this boldly. An artist is proud of his workshop
    When he looks round it and sees such an assembly of gods.   240
Jupiter bows his majestic head, and Juno holds hers high;
    Phoebus Apollo strides forth, shaking the locks from his brow;
And Minerva looks sternly down—and here's light-footed Hermes
    Casting a sidelong glance, roguish, yet tender as well.
But on soft Bacchus, the dreamer, the gaze of the lovely Cythere
    Falls with sweet longing; her eyes even in marble are moist.
She remembers his ardent embrace, and seems to be asking:
    'Where is our glorious son? Here at our side he should stand!'

XIV

Hörest du, Liebchen, das muntre Geschrei den Flaminischen
    Weg her?
    Schnitter sind es; sie ziehn wieder nach Hause zurück,   250
Weit hinweg. Sie haben des Römers Ernte vollendet,
    Der für Ceres den Kranz selber zu flechten verschmäht.
Keine Feste sind mehr der großen Göttin gewidmet,
    Die, statt Eicheln, zur Kost goldenen Weizen verlieh.
Laß uns beide das Fest im stillen freudig begehen!
    Sind zwei Liebende doch sich ein versammeltes Volk.
Hast du wohl je gehört von jener mystischen Feier,
    Die von Eleusis hieher frühe dem Sieger gefolgt?
Griechen stifteten sie, und immer riefen nur Griechen,
    Selbst in den Mauern Roms: 'Kommt zur geheiligten Nacht!'   260
Fern entwich der Profane; da bebte der wartende Neuling,
    Den ein weißes Gewand, Zeichen der Reinheit, umgab.
Wunderlich irrte darauf der Eingeführte durch Kreise
    Seltner Gestalten; im Traum schien er zu wallen: denn hier
Wanden sich Schlangen am Boden umher, verschlossene
    Kästchen,
    Reich mit Ähren umkränzt, trugen hier Mädchen vorbei,
Vielbedeutend gebärdeten sich die Priester und summten;
    Ungeduldig und bang harrte der Lehrling auf Licht.
Erst nach mancherlei Proben und Prüfungen ward ihm enthüllet,
    Was der geheiligte Kreis seltsam in Bildern verbarg.   270
Und was war das Geheimnis! als daß Demeter, die große,
    Sich gefällig einmal auch einem Helden bequemt,

XIV

Do you hear, darling, the merry shouts from the Via Flaminia?*
  Those are the homeward bound reapers—their journey was
    long,   250
Coming to gather the Roman harvest, coming to crown great
  Ceres* with garlands, a task which our own citizens scorn.
For that goddess is honoured with feasts no longer, whose bounty
  Bettered our acorn fare, gave us the gold of her wheat.
So let us gladly, you and I, do her homage in private:
  Surely two partners in love are a whole nation in joy!
Have you perhaps heard tell of those ancient mystical rites which
  Followed the Conqueror's path, back from Eleusis* to Rome?
They had been founded by Greeks, and even here in this city
  Those were still Greeks who cried: 'This is the holy night,
    come!'   260
Then the profane would depart, and the waiting novice would
    tremble,
  Clad, as befitting the pure, in his white candidate's robe.
Strangely the newcomer wandered then, encircled by figures
  Strange to behold—he walked as in a dream-world: for here
Serpents writhed on the ground around him, and young girls
    passed him—
  Close-locked caskets they bore, richly with corn-ears wreathed;
Priests mysteriously moved and chanted in rites full of meaning;
  Here the learner in awe eagerly waited for light.
Not until after much testing and many ordeals did they teach him
  What in that circle, in signs wondrous and sacred, lay hid.   270
And what was the great secret? No more than that mighty
    Demeter,
  She too, once, had obliged, bowed to a hero's desire—

Als sie Jasion einst, dem rüstigen König der Kreter,
  Ihres unsterblichen Leibs holdes Verborgne gegönnt.
Da war Kreta beglückt! das Hochzeitbette der Göttin
  Schwoll von Ähren, und reich drückte den Acker die Saat.
Aber die übrige Welt verschmachtete; denn es versäumte
  Über der Liebe Genuß Ceres den schönen Beruf.
Voll Erstaunen vernahm der Eingeweihte das Märchen,
  Winkte der Liebsten — Verstehst du nun, Geliebte, den Wink?   280
Jene buschige Myrte beschattet ein heiliges Plätzchen!
  Unsre Zufriedenheit bringt keine Gefährde der Welt.

When long ago to the stalwart Jasion,* king of the Cretans,
 She disclosed her divine limbs and their hidden delights.
Fortunate Crete! for that island, the wedding-couch of the
  goddess,
 Teemed with corn from then on, heavy its fields were with
  wheat,
But all the rest of the world had to languish, for Ceres neglected
 In the enjoyment of love what she was wont to provide.
And the initiate, amazed on hearing this tale, made a signal
 To his beloved—do you, darling, know now what it meant? 280
Look, there's a sacred spot which those myrtle-bushes are hiding:
 We can be happy in there, and not endanger mankind.

XV

Amor bleibet ein Schalk, und wer ihm vertraut, ist betrogen!
    Heuchelnd kam er zu mir: 'Diesmal nur traue mir noch.
Redlich mein ichs mit dir: du hast dein Leben und Dichten,
    Dankbar erkenn ich es wohl, meiner Verehrung geweiht.
Siehe, dir bin ich nun gar nach Rom gefolget; ich möchte
    Dir im fremden Gebiet gern was Gefälliges tun.
Jeder Reisende klagt, er finde schlechte Bewirtung;
    Welchen Amor empfiehlt, köstlich bewirtet ist er.   290
Du betrachtest mit Staunen die Trümmern alter Gebäude
    Und durchwandelst mit Sinn diesen geheiligten Raum.
Du verehrest noch mehr die werten Reste des Bildens
    Einziger Künstler, die stets ich in der Werkstatt besucht.
Diese Gestalten, ich formte sie selbst! Verzeih mir, ich prahle
    Diesmal nicht; du gestehst, was ich dir sage, sei wahr.
Nun du mir lässiger dienst, wo sind die schönen Gestalten,
    Wo die Farben, der Glanz deiner Erfindungen hin?
Denkst du nun wieder zu bilden, o Freund? Die Schule der
       Griechen
    Blieb noch offen, das Tor schlossen die Jahre nicht zu.   300
Ich, der Lehrer, bin ewig jung, und liebe die Jungen.
    Altklug lieb ich dich nicht! Munter! Begreife mich wohl!
War das Antike doch neu, da jene Glücklichen lebten!
    Lebe glücklich, und so lebe die Vorzeit in dir!
Stoff zum Liede, wo nimmst du ihn her? Ich muß dir ihn geben,
    Und den höheren Stil lehret die Liebe dich nur.'

XV*

Eros was ever a rogue, and his promises fool the unwary.
    Subtly dissembling he came: 'Trust me just this once!' he said,
'I mean well by you—you have devoted your life and your
        writings
    To my service and fame, and this I gratefully note.
Now, having followed you even to Rome, as you see, in this
        foreign
    Country I should, in some way, like to do you a good turn.
Travellers always complain they are not treated as a guest should
        be;
    But they get all they could wish when they are sponsored by
        Love.   290
Here you stare with amazement at ancient buildings in ruins,
    And in this sacred place thoughtful and curious you roam;
Even more you revere the noble fragments of certain
    Rare creators, whom I often would visit at work—
For it was I who shaped and created for them! Forgive me,
    This is no idle boast; you must acknowledge its truth.
Since you became more lax in my service, have not your
        inventions
    Lost all their colour and form, lustre and beauty? My friend,
Would you now practise your art once more? The school of the
        Greeks is
    Open as ever; the years pass, yet its doors never closed.   300
I, the teacher, can never grow old; I love all who are youthful—
    Lively of heart, young in mind! be so, and mark my words well:
When they lived and enjoyed, it was new, that world you call
        ancient:
    Now, by enjoying your life, make the past live on in you!
Where shall you find a theme for your songs? It is Love who
        provides it,
    And in the loftier style there's no tuition like mine.'

Also sprach der Sophist. Wer widerspräch ihm? und leider
  Bin ich zu folgen gewöhnt, wenn der Gebieter befiehlt. —
Nun, verräterisch hält er sein Wort, gibt Stoff zu Gesängen,
  Ach! und raubt mir die Zeit, Kraft und Besinnung zugleich;   310
Blick und Händedruck, und Küsse, gemütliche Worte,
  Silben köstlichen Sinns wechselt ein liebendes Paar.
Da wird Lispeln Geschwätz, wird Stottern liebliche Rede:
  Solch ein Hymnus verhallt ohne prosodisches Maß.
Dich, Aurora, wie kannt ich dich sonst als Freundin der Musen!
  Hat, Aurora, dich auch Amor, der lose, verführt?
Du erscheinest mir nun als seine Freundin, und weckest
  Mich an seinem Altar wieder zum festlichen Tag.
Find ich die Fülle der Locken an meinem Busen! Das Köpfchen
  Ruhet und drücket den Arm, der sich dem Halse bequemt.   320
Welch ein freudig Erwachen! Erhieltet ihr ruhige Stunden
  Mir das Denkmal der Lust, die in den Schlaf uns gewiegt? —
Sie bewegt sich im Schlummer und sinkt auf die Breite des Lagers,
  Weggewendet; und doch läßt sie mir Hand noch in Hand.
Herzliche Liebe verbindet uns stets und treues Verlangen,
  Und den Wechsel behielt nur die Begierde sich vor.
Einen Druck der Hand, ich sehe die himmlischen Augen
  Wieder offen. — O nein! laßt auf der Bildung mich ruhn!
Bleibt geschlossen! ihr macht mich verwirrt und trunken, ihr
    raubet
  Mir den stillen Genuß reiner Betrachtung zu früh.   330
Diese Formen, wie groß! wie edel gewendet die Glieder!
  Schlief Ariadne so schön: Theseus, du konntest entfliehn?
Diesen Lippen ein einziger Kuß! O Theseus, nun scheide!
  Blick ihr ins Auge! Sie wacht! — Ewig nun hält sie dich fest.

Thus this sophist addressed me; and who should gainsay him?
    Alas, I
  Only too gladly obey when I receive his commands.
Well, he is true to his word, yet false! I have matter for poems;
    But where, alas, is my time, where are my senses and strength?   310
Now two lovers, with pressure of hands, with glances and kisses,
    Murmur in tender exchange syllables precious to hear.
Lisping and stammering turn into talk, into sweetest of converse—
    Rhapsodies, hymns of a kind, but not the kind you can scan.
Goddess of Dawn, hitherto I have known you as 'friend of the
    Muses'!*
  Have Love's blandishing wiles won the dawn-goddess as well?
Now you come to my window as *his* paramour, and I waken
    Here at his altar again, greeting the splendour of day.
Over my breast her locks fall full and abundant; her head droops
    Heavy, her neck fits snug on my encircling arm.   320
Here's an awakening indeed! Have these quiet hours preserved you,
    Has your memorial been raised,* pleasure that rocked us to sleep?
In her slumber she moves and turns away from me, sinks down
    On the wide bed, but her hand still she leaves lying in mine.
Tenderest love is the bond between us, and faithfullest longing;
    Only our mutual desire varies, as appetites do.
If I so much as press on her hand, I shall see her enchanting
    Eyes reopen—ah no! let me still study her shape!
Eyes, stay closed! you make me confused and drunken, too soon
    you
  Bring to an end this pure, quiet, contemplative joy.   330
Look, how splendid these forms, how nobly moulded her limbs are!
    Did Ariadne* sleep so? Theseus, oh how could you leave?
Only one kiss on those lovely lips—flee, Theseus! she wakes! Now
    You are her captive—her gaze holds you for ever in thrall.

XVI

Zünde mir Licht an, Knabe! — 'Noch ist es hell. Ihr verzehret
   Öl und Docht nur umsonst. Schließet die Läden doch nicht!
Hinter die Häuser entwich, nicht hinter den Berg, uns die Sonne!
   Ein halb Stündchen noch währts bis zum Geläute der Nacht.' —
Unglückseliger! geh und gehorch! Mein Mädchen erwart ich.
   Tröste mich, Lämpchen, indes, lieblicher Bote der Nacht!   340

XVI

Light the lamp for me, boy!—'But it's daylight still! you are
    wasting
  Oil and wick, sir, in vain. Why close the shutters just yet?
Look, the sun is not under the hill, only under the housetops!
  There'll be another half-hour yet till the angelus rings.'
Wretch! obey me at once! My beloved is coming!—And
    meanwhile,
  Till she is here, little lamp, comfort me, herald of night!   340

XVII

Zwei gefährliche Schlangen, vom Chore der Dichter gescholten,
    Grausend nennt sie die Welt Jahre die tausende schon,
Python, dich, und dich, Lernäischer Drache! Doch seid ihr
    Durch die rüstige Hand tätiger Götter gefällt.
Ihr zerstöret nicht mehr mit feurigem Atem und Geifer
    Herde, Wiesen und Wald, goldene Saaten nicht mehr.
Doch welch ein feindlicher Gott hat uns im Zorne die neue
    Ungeheure Geburt giftigen Schlammes gesandt?
Überall schleicht er sich ein, und in den lieblichsten Gärtchen
    Lauert tückisch der Wurm, packt den Genießenden an.   350
Sei mir, hesperischer Drache, gegrüßt, du zeigtest dich mutig,
    Du verteidigtest kühn goldener Äpfel Besitz!
Aber dieser verteidiget nichts — und wo er sich findet,
    Sind die Gärten, die Frucht keiner Verteidigung wert.
Heimlich krümmet er sich im Busche, besudelt die Quellen,
    Geifert, wandelt in Gift Amors belebenden Tau.
O! wie glücklich warst du, Lucrez! du konntest der Liebe
    Ganz entsagen und dich jeglichem Körper vertraun.
Selig warst du, Properz! dir holte der Sklave die Dirnen
    Vom Aventinus herab, aus dem Tarpeischen Hain.   360
Und wenn Cynthia dich aus jenen Umarmungen schreckte,
    Untreu fand sie dich zwar; aber sie fand dich gesund.
Jetzt wer hütet sich nicht, langweilige Treue zu brechen!
    Wen die Liebe nicht hält, hält die Besorglichkeit auf.
Und auch da, wer weiß! gewagt ist jegliche Freude,
    Nirgend legt man das Haupt ruhig dem Weib in den Schoß.
Sicher ist nicht das Ehbett mehr, nicht sicher der Ehbruch;
    Gatte, Gattin und Freund, eins ist im andern verletzt.
O! der goldenen Zeit! da Jupiter noch, vom Olympus,
    Sich zu Semele bald, bald zu Kallisto begab.   370

XVII

You were two perilous serpents, reviled with one voice by the
  poets,
  And for long ages the world shuddered on hearing your names:
Python,* and you, Lernaean Hydra!* But luckily you're both
  Dead, struck down by the strong hands of adventuresome gods.
Now your fiery breath and your venomous spittle no longer
  Blast our forests and flocks, blight our rich acres of corn.
But, alas! what god in his fury and malice has sent us
  This new monster,* this plague born of the poisonous mire?
Nowhere is safe from its creeping intrusion, it lurks in the
  loveliest
  Gardens, this treacherous worm strikes in the act of our joy!   350
Hail, Hesperian dragon!* at least you bravely and fiercely
  Guarded those apples of gold, out in the uttermost west.
But this creature has nothing to guard, for gardens where he hides,
  And any fruit he has touched, they're not worth guarding at all.
Secretly there in the bushes he squirms, befouling the waters,
  Slavering poison and death into Love's life-giving dew.
Happy Lucretius!* you could renounce romantic attachment,
  And without cause for alarm clasp any body you chose.
Slaves brought you your consenting bedmates, lucky Propertius,*
  Down from the Aventine Hill, out of the Tarpeian Grove;   360
And if Cynthia caught you with one, then though you had
  wronged her
  By being faithless, at least nothing was wrong with your health.
Who does not hesitate now to break faith with a tedious mistress?
  Love may not hold us, but sheer caution will make us think
  twice.
Even at home, who knows! Not a single pleasure is risk-free;
  Who in his own wife's lap now lays a confident head?
Neither in wedlock now nor out of it can we be certain;
  Mutually noxious we are, husband and lover and wife.
Oh for that golden age, when Jove would descend from Olympus,
  Visiting Semele's* place, paying Callisto* a call!   370

Ihm lag selber daran, die Schwelle des heiligen Tempels
   Rein zu finden, den er liebend und mächtig betrat.
O! wie hätte Juno getobt, wenn im Streite der Liebe
   Gegen sie der Gemahl giftige Waffen gekehrt.
Doch wir sind nicht so ganz, wir alte Heiden, verlassen,
   Immer schwebet ein Gott über der Erde noch hin,
Eilig und geschäftig, ihr kennt ihn alle, verehrt ihn!
   Ihn den Boten des Zeus, Hermes, den heilenden Gott.
Fielen des Vaters Tempel zu Grund, bezeichnen die Säulen
   Paarweis kaum noch den Platz alter verehrender Pracht,   380
Wird des Sohnes Tempel doch stehn und ewige Zeiten
   Wechselt der Bittende stets dort mit dem Dankenden ab.
Eins nur fleh ich im stillen, an euch ihr Grazien wend ich
   Dieses heiße Gebet tief aus dem Busen herauf:
Schützet immer mein kleines, mein artiges Gärtchen, entfernet
   Jegliches Übel von mir; reichet mir Amor die Hand,
O! so gebet mir stets, sobald ich dem Schelmen vertraue,
   Ohne Sorgen und Furcht, ohne Gefahr den Genuß.

He himself, in that sacred temple, required a clean welcome
   When he came to its door, entering in amorous might.
What a great fuss would Juno* have made, if she'd found that
      with poisoned
   Weapons her husband fought, back in the conjugal bed!—
But we old heathen sinners are not completely abandoned;
   We can still call on one god—he hovers over the earth,
Busy and swift: you all know his name, so pay him due homage!
   He, Jove's messenger-boy, Mercury—he knows the cure.*
Though his father's great temples have fallen, with pairs of old
      columns
   Scarcely still marking the place of the majestic old cult,   380
Yet young Mercury's temple will stand, and his suppliants enter
   Still, while others depart gratefully, world without end.
One petition to you, oh Graces, I offer in private!
   Grant this one fervent request, made from the depths of my
      heart:
Always protect the neat little garden I cherish, and always
   Fend off diseases from me; when I'm invited by Love
And when I trust myself to him, that rogue, may my pleasure
      be ever
   Carefree, and never with fear, never with danger be mixed!

XVIII

Cäsarn wär ich wohl nie zu fernen Britannen gefolget,
    Florus hätte mich leicht in die Popine geschleppt!   390
Denn mir bleiben weit mehr die Nebel des traurigen Nordens,
    Als ein geschäftiges Volk südlicher Flöhe verhaßt.
Und noch schöner von heut an seid mir gegrüßet, ihr Schenken,
    Osterien, wie euch schicklich der Römer benennt;
Denn ihr zeigtet mir heute die Liebste, begleitet vom Oheim,
    Den die Gute so oft, mich zu besitzen, betriegt.
Hier stand unser Tisch, den Deutsche vertraulich umgaben;
    Drüben suchte das Kind neben der Mutter den Platz,
Rückte vielmals die Bank und wußt es artig zu machen,
    Daß ich halb ihr Gesicht, völlig den Nacken gewann.   400
Lauter sprach sie, als hier die Römerin pfleget, kredenzte,
    Blickte gewendet nach mir, goß und verfehlte das Glas.
Wein floß über den Tisch, und sie, mit zierlichem Finger,
    Zog auf dem hölzernen Blatt Kreise der Feuchtigkeit hin.
Meinen Namen verschlang sie dem ihrigen; immer begierig
    Schaut ich dem Fingerchen nach, und sie bemerkte mich wohl.
Endlich zog sie behende das Zeichen der römischen Fünfe
    Und ein Strichlein davor. Schnell, und sobald ichs gesehn,
Schlang sie Kreise durch Kreise, die Lettern und Ziffern zu
       löschen;
    Aber die köstliche *Vier* blieb mir ins Auge geprägt.   410
Stumm war ich sitzen geblieben, und biß die glühende Lippe,
    Halb aus Schalkheit und Lust, halb aus Begierde, mir wund.
Erst noch so lange bis Nacht! dann noch vier Stunden zu warten!
    Hohe Sonne, du weilst, und du beschauest dein Rom!
Größeres sahest du nichts und wirst nichts Größeres sehen,
    Wie es dein Priester Horaz in der Entzückung versprach.
Aber heute verweile mir nicht, und wende die Blicke
    Von dem Siebengebirg früher und williger ab!

XVIII

Caesar would hardly have got me to travel to far-away Britain;
  Florus's* taverns in Rome would have been more to my taste. 390
If one must choose between mists of the dismal north and a host
    of
  Hard-working southern fleas, give me the fleas any day!
And I have now even greater cause to salute and to praise you,
  Osterie*—as inns here are so fittingly called:
For my darling today came to one of you, brought by her uncle,*
  Whom so often she tricks when she finds ways to meet me.
Here was our table, with its familiar circle of Germans;
  And at a table near by, next to her mother, she sat.
Clever girl! she shifted the bench and so rearranged things
  That I could half see her face, and her whole neck was in view. 400
Raising her voice rather high for a Roman girl, she did the
    honours,
  Gave me a sidelong look, poured the wine, missing her glass.
Over the table it spilled,* and with dainty finger she doodled—
  There, on the wet wooden page, circles of moisture she traced.
My name she mingled with hers; I eagerly followed her finger,
  Watching its every stroke, and she well knew that I did.
Quickly at last she inscribed a Roman 'five', with an upright
  'One' in front of it—then, when I had seen this, at once
With arabesque-like lines she effaced the letters and numbers,
  But left stamped on my mind's eye the delectable 'IV'.* 410
I had sat speechless, biting my burning lip till it bled; half
  Mischievous pleasure I felt, half was aflame with desire.
Still so long until nightfall, and four more hours then of waiting!
  High sun, pausing to gaze down at your city of Rome,
Nothing you ever have seen has been greater, and nothing you
    will see;
  This was the truth that your priest, Horace, in rapture
    foretold.*
Only today do not linger, consent to be brief in your survey,
  Sooner than usual to take leave of the fair Seven Hills!

Einem Dichter zuliebe verkürze die herrlichen Stunden,
   Die mit begierigem Blick selig der Maler genießt;   420
Glühend blicke noch schnell zu diesen hohen Fassaden,
   Kuppeln und Säulen zuletzt und Obelisken herauf;
Stürze dich eilig ins Meer, um morgen früher zu sehen,
   Was Jahrhunderte schon göttliche Lust dir gewährt:
Diese feuchten, mit Rohr so lange bewachsnen Gestade,
   Diese mit Bäumen und Busch düster beschatteten Höhn.
Wenig Hütten zeigten sie erst; dann sahst du auf einmal
   Sie vom wimmelnden Volk glücklicher Räuber belebt.
Alles schleppten sie drauf an diese Stätte zusammen;
   Kaum war das übrige Rund deiner Betrachtung noch wert.   430
Sahst eine Welt hier entstehn, sahst dann eine Welt hier in
      Trümmern,
   Aus den Trümmern aufs neu fast eine größere Welt!
Daß ich diese noch lange von dir beleuchtet erblicke,
   Spinne die Parze mir klug langsam den Faden herab.
Aber sie eile herbei, die schön bezeichnete Stunde! —
   Glücklich! hör ich sie schon? Nein; doch ich höre schon Drei.
So, ihr lieben Musen, betrogt ihr wieder die Länge
   Dieser Weile, die mich von der Geliebten getrennt.
Lebet wohl! Nun eil ich, und fürcht euch nicht zu beleidigen;
   Denn ihr Stolzen, ihr gebt Amorn doch immer den Rang.   440

Show a poet this favour, and shorten the hours of splendid
 Brightness, which painters' eyes drink so insatiably in; 420
Flash but a farewell glance at these lofty façades, at these columns;
 Gleam on the obelisks, gleam now on the domes, and begone!
Swiftly plunge into the sea and rise early tomorrow to hasten
 Back to this ageless sight, feast for the gaze of a god.
See, these moist river-banks that so long were covered with
  rushes,
 And these dark wooded hills, shadowed with bushes and
  trees—
Only a few huts stood there at first, then a flourishing tribe of
 Fortunate robbers* arrived, peopling the place in a trice.
Here they gathered, and here their loot and wealth they
  assembled;
 This you observed—little else seemed to you worthy of note. 430
This was the birth of a world, and you saw it then perish in ruins,
 But from the ruins perhaps something still greater arose.
Oh, that I yet may for long behold this world in your radiance,
 Wisely and slow let the Fates spin out the thread of my life!
But that hour she so sweetly assigned, oh, let it come quickly!
 Does it already strike four? No; but with joy I hear three.
So, dear Muses, once more, as the tedious hours divided
 Me from my darling, how well you have beguiled them away!
Farewell now! I'll make haste to my tryst, and not fear to offend
  you;
 You may be proud, but you grant precedence always to Love. 440

XIX

'Warum bist du, Geliebter, nicht heute zur Vigne gekommen?
   Einsam, wie ich versprach, wartet ich oben auf dich.' —
Beste, schon war ich hinein; da sah ich zum Glücke den Oheim
   Neben den Stöcken, bemüht, hin sich und her sich zu drehn.
Schleichend eilt ich hinaus! — 'O welch ein Irrtum ergriff dich!
   Eine Scheuche nur wars, was dich vertrieb! Die Gestalt
Flickten wir emsig zusammen aus alten Kleidern und Rohren;
   Emsig half ich daran, selbst mir zu schaden bemüht.' —
Nun, des Alten Wunsch ist erfüllt; den losesten Vogel
   Scheucht' er heute, der ihm Gärtchen und Nichte bestiehlt.   450

XIX*

'Darling, why didn't you come today to the vineyard to meet me?
  I waited there by myself, just as I promised I would!'
'Sweetheart, I came—but just then, by good luck, I caught sight
    of your uncle
  Busily watching the vines, turning his head to and fro;
So I crept out again quickly!' 'My dear, what a silly mistake!
    That's
  Only the scarecrow—so that scared you away! We all worked
Stitching the dummy together with sticks and old clothes, and I
    helped too
  Making it. So all that work brought me bad luck in the end!'
Well, the old man should be glad today to have startled a bird
    more
  Wanton than any, whose wiles steal both his fruit and his niece. 450

XX

Manche Töne sind mir Verdruß, doch bleibet am meisten
   Hundegebell mir verhaßt; kläffend zerreißt es mein Ohr.
Einen Hund nur hör ich sehr oft mit frohem Behagen
   Bellend kläffen, den Hund, den sich der Nachbar erzog.
Denn er bellte mir einst mein Mädchen an, da sie sich heimlich
   Zu mir stahl, und verriet unser Geheimnis beinah.
Jetzo, hör ich ihn bellen, so denk ich mir immer: sie kommt wohl!
   Oder ich denke der Zeit, da die Erwartete kam.

XX

Many noises enrage me, but none, I think, is more odious
  Than the barking, the ear-splintering yapping of dogs.
Only my neighbour's dog is now an exception: so often
  Hearing his bark and his yelp, I am contented and glad.
For he barked at my darling once, when secretly she was
  Stealing a visit to me, and nearly gave us away.
Now, if I hear him bark, I always think: she must be coming!
  Or I remember the time when, long-awaited, she came.

XXI

Eines ist mir verdrießlich vor allen Dingen, ein andres
    Bleibt mir abscheulich, empört jegliche Faser in mir,   460
Nur der bloße Gedanke. Ich will es euch, Freunde, gestehen:
    Gar verdrießlich ist mir einsam das Lager zu Nacht.
Aber ganz abscheulich ists, auf dem Wege der Liebe
    Schlangen zu fürchten, und Gift unter den Rosen der Lust,
Wenn im schönsten Moment der hin sich gebenden Freude
    Deinem sinkenden Haupt lispelnde Sorge sich naht.
Darum macht Faustine mein Glück; sie teilet das Lager
    Gerne mit mir, und bewahrt Treue dem Treuen genau.
Reizendes Hindernis will die rasche Jugend; ich liebe,
    Mich des versicherten Guts lange bequem zu erfreun.   470
Welche Seligkeit ists! wir wechseln sichere Küsse,
    Atem und Leben getrost saugen und flößen wir ein.
So erfreuen wir uns der langen Nächte, wir lauschen,
    Busen an Busen gedrängt, Stürmen und Regen und Guß.
Und so dämmert der Morgen heran; es bringen die Stunden
    Neue Blumen herbei, schmücken uns festlich den Tag.
Gönnet mir, o Quiriten! das Glück, und jedem gewähre
    Aller Güter der Welt erstes und letztes der Gott!

XXI

One thing I find more irksome than anything else, and another
    Thing I supremely abhor—it really curdles my blood,   460
Even the thought of it does. Let me tell you, my friends, what
    these two are:
   First, to sleep by myself irks me, I truly confess.
But what I utterly loathe is the fear that on pathways of pleasure,
    Under the roses of love, serpents and poison* may lurk.
This is the hideous thought which at moments of sweetest
    surrender,
   As I half swoon with delight, care whispers into my ear.
That is what makes me so happy to have Faustina: she gladly
    Sleeps with me, but she remains faithful, as I do to her.
Risks and checks may attract impetuous youth, but for my part
    Let me in comfort possess what is reliably mine.   470
What delight for us both! We kiss with confidence, safely
    Breathe the other's breath in, suck the dear life each from each.
Thus we enjoy the long nights together, we lie and we listen,
    Heart pressed to heart, as the wind storms and the rain gushes
    down,
Till dawn breaks, and the morning shines on us. Thus, as they
    pass, new
   Festive blossoms adorn every new hour of our day.
Oh, Rome's citizens, do not begrudge me such bliss! and to all
    men
   May Love grant it—this first, this crowning blessing of life.

XXII

Schwer erhalten wir uns den guten Namen, denn Fama
  Steht mit Amorn, ich weiß, meinem Gebieter, in Streit.   480
Wißt auch ihr, woher es entsprang, daß beide sich hassen?
  Alte Geschichten sind das, und ich erzähle sie wohl.
Immer die mächtige Göttin, doch war sie für die Gesellschaft
  Unerträglich, denn gern führt sie das herrschende Wort;
Und so war sie von je, bei allen Göttergelagen,
  Mit der Stimme von Erz, Großen und Kleinen verhaßt.
So berühmte sie einst sich übermütig, sie habe
  Jovis herrlichen Sohn ganz sich zum Sklaven gemacht.
'Meinen Herkules führ ich dereinst, o Vater der Götter',
  Rief triumphierend sie aus, 'wiedergeboren dir zu.   490
Herkules ist es nicht mehr, den dir Alkmene geboren;
  Seine Verehrung für mich macht ihn auf Erden zum Gott.
Schaut er nach dem Olymp, so glaubst du, er schaue nach deinen
  Mächtigen Knieen; vergib! nur in den Äther nach mir
Blickt der würdigste Mann; nur mich zu verdienen, durchschreitet
  Leicht sein mächtiger Fuß Bahnen, die keiner betrat;
Aber auch ich begegn ihm auf seinen Wegen, und preise
  Seinen Namen voraus, eh er die Tat noch beginnt.
Mich vermählst du ihm einst; der Amazonen Besieger
  Werd auch meiner, und ihn nenn ich mit Freuden Gemahl!'   500
Alles schwieg; sie mochten nicht gern die Prahlerin reizen:
  Denn sie denkt sich, erzürnt, leicht was Gehässiges aus.
Amorn bemerkte sie nicht: er schlich beiseite; den Helden
  Bracht er mit weniger Kunst unter der Schönsten Gewalt.
Nun vermummt er sein Paar: ihr hängt er die Bürde des Löwen
  Über die Schultern und lehnt mühsam die Keule dazu,
Drauf bespickt er mit Blumen des Helden sträubende Haare,
  Reichet den Rocken der Faust, die sich dem Scherze bequemt.
So vollendet er bald die neckische Gruppe; dann läuft er,
  Ruft durch den ganzen Olymp: 'Herrliche Taten geschehn!   510

XXII

Our good name is in danger, I fear; between Love who commands
  me
  And the goddess Repute* there is, I know, bitter strife.   480
And have you heard how it all began, that mutual hatred?
  It's an old story, you see, one that I might as well tell.
She is indeed a powerful goddess, but socially she was
  Quite impossible—too talkative, rasping away
With her clangorous voice—and each time the gods were
  assembled,
  All of them, great and small, heartily hated its sound.
Thus in her arrogance once she boasted as one of her conquests
  Jove's magnificent son: 'Hercules* now is my slave,*
Father Jupiter!' proudly she cried, 'and one day I shall bring him
  Up to Olympus with me, totally mine and reborn!   490
He is no longer Alcmene's* son, the hero you fathered;
  His devotion to me makes him a god upon earth.
When he looks up at us, not Jove's mighty knees are attracting
  His rapt gaze, as you think: no, excuse me! it is I
Whom this noblest of men looks heavenwards for, only I whom
  He would deserve as he strides paths no one else ever trod.
But I meet him as well on his ways, I go forward before him,
  Praising his name as he comes, heralding deeds still undone.
I shall demand him from you in marriage: the Amazon's victor*
  Shall be mine also—with joy I shall be Hercules' wife!'   500
All were silent, for none of them felt like provoking the
  loudmouth:
  When she is angered, her spite quickly breeds slanderous tales.
Only Eros evaded her notice by stealth; and with ease he
  Soon had her hero bewitched, to a fair lady* enthralled.
Then he transvested the pair, laboriously laying the lion's
  Pelt across Omphale's back, putting the club by her side.
Next, with flowers he decked the resisting hair of the hero—
  But with a distaff in hand, Hercules joined in the joke.
Thus the Love-god completed this teasing pose, and ran swiftly
  Through the Olympian halls, crying: 'Great deeds! Come and
  see!   510

Nie hat Erd und Himmel, die unermüdete Sonne
   Hat auf der ewigen Bahn keines der Wunder erblickt.'
Alles eilte; sie glaubten dem losen Knaben, denn ernstlich
   Hatt er gesprochen; und auch Fama, sie blieb nicht zurück.
Wer sich freute, den Mann so tief erniedrigt zu sehen,
   Denkt ihr! Juno. Es galt Amorn ein freundlich Gesicht.
Fama daneben, wie stand sie beschämt, verlegen, verzweifelnd!
   Anfangs lachte sie nur: 'Masken, ihr Götter, sind das!
Meinen Helden, ich kenn ihn zu gut! Es haben Tragöden
   Uns zum besten!' Doch bald sah sie mit Schmerzen, er wars! — 520
Nicht den tausendsten Teil verdroß es Vulkanen, sein Weibchen
   Mit dem rüstigen Freund unter den Maschen zu sehn,
Als das verständige Netz im rechten Moment sie umfaßte,
   Rasch die Verschlungnen umschlang, fest die Genießenden
      hielt.
Wie sich die Jünglinge freuten! Merkur und Bacchus! sie beide
   Mußten gestehn: es sei, über dem Busen zu ruhn
Dieses herrlichen Weibes, ein schöner Gedanke. Sie baten:
   Löse, Vulkan, sie noch nicht! Laß sie noch einmal besehn.
Und der Alte war so Hahnrei, und hielt sie nur fester. —
   Aber Fama, sie floh rasch und voll Grimmes davon.   530
Seit der Zeit ist zwischen den zweien der Fehde nicht Stillstand;
   Wie sie sich Helden erwählt, gleich ist der Knabe darnach.
Wer sie am höchsten verehrt, den weiß er am besten zu fassen,
   Und den Sittlichsten greift er am gefährlichsten an.
Will ihm einer entgehn, den bringt er vom Schlimmen ins
      Schlimmste.
   Mädchen bietet er an; wer sie ihm töricht verschmäht,
Muß erst grimmige Pfeile von seinem Bogen erdulden;
   Mann erhitzt er auf Mann, treibt die Begierden aufs Tier.
Wer sich seiner schämt, der muß erst leiden; dem Heuchler
   Streut er bittern Genuß unter Verbrechen und Not.   540

Never has heaven or earth or the tireless sun on its endless
    Course seen a wonder to beat this one that I'll show you now!'
And they all came, for the words of the mischievous knave had
      been earnest,
    So they believed him; and she, Reputation, came with them as
      well.
Guess who was glad to behold her husband's bastard so humbled!
    Juno, of course; and on Love now she most graciously smiled.
But Reputation stood there ashamed, embarrassed, despairing.
    First she tried laughing it off: 'Gods, these are nothing but
      masks!
I know my hero only too well: we are being made fools of
    By mere actors!' But soon, stricken, she saw she was wrong!—   520
Vulcan* had felt not a thousandth part of her rage when he found
    his
    Wife with her martial friend, caught in the net on their bed,
By his cunning invention enmeshed at just the right moment,
    Clasped in it as they lay clutched, locked in their spasm of joy.
How that had pleased young Bacchus and Mercury! Both had
      admitted
    What a fine thing it would be, if one could lie for a while
In the embrace of that lovely goddess. They had asked Vulcan:
    'Don't release her just yet! Let's have another good look!'
And the old man, having nothing to lose, kept his cuckolders
      captive.—
    But Reputation now fled furiously from the scene;   530
And ever since, she and Love have constantly warred with each
      other.
    Heroes whom she singles out, he at once marks for attack;
Those who are most devoted to her are the boy's surest victims,
    And the strict moralists, their peril is greater by far.
All who would flee from him fare the worst with this maker of
      mischief:
    Girls he will offer them—if these they imprudently scorn,
Then indeed he will pierce their pride with his angriest arrows:
    Male he inflames for male, drives us to lust after beasts.
All who feel shame about Love he punishes: hypocrites have to
    Burn with bitter desires, driven to crime and despair.   540

Aber auch sie, die Göttin, verfolgt ihn mit Augen und Ohren;
 Sieht sie ihn einmal bei dir, gleich ist sie feindlich gesinnt,
Schreckt dich mit ernstem Blick, verachtenden Mienen, und heftig
 Strenge verruft sie das Haus, das er gewöhnlich besucht.
Und so geht es auch mir: schon leid ich ein wenig; die Göttin,
 Eifersüchtig, sie forscht meinem Geheimnisse nach.
Doch es ist ein altes Gesetz: ich schweig und verehre;
 Denn der Könige Zwist büßten die Griechen, wie ich.

But Reputation pursues him too with sharpest of ears and
    Eyes: beware of her wrath if she once finds him with you!
Her stern looks and contempt will startle you—with a fierce rigour
    Fame will defame any house visited often by Love.
I too am learning this now, and the jealous goddess already
    Plagues me a little: she spies out my most secret delights.
So the old rule holds good—I revere it in silence: for 'when their
    Mad kings quarrelled, the Greeks paid for it';* so too with me.

XXIII

Zieret Stärke den Mann und freies mutiges Wesen,
    Oh! so ziemet ihm fast tiefes Geheimnis noch mehr.   550
Städtebezwingerin du, Verschwiegenheit! Fürstin der Völker!
    Teure Göttin, die mich sicher durchs Leben geführt,
Welches Schicksal erfahr ich! Es löset scherzend die Muse,
    Amor löset, der Schalk, mir den verschlossenen Mund.
Ach, schon wird es so schwer, der Könige Schande verbergen!
    Weder die Krone bedeckt, weder ein phrygischer Bund
Midas' verlängertes Ohr; der nächste Diener entdeckt es,
    Und ihm ängstet und drückt gleich das Geheimnis die Brust.
In die Erde vergrüb er es gern, um sich zu erleichtern:
    Doch die Erde verwahrt solche Geheimnisse nicht;   560
Rohre sprießen hervor und rauschen und lispeln im Winde:
    Midas! Midas, der Fürst, trägt ein verlängertes Ohr!
Schwerer wird es nun mir, ein schönes Geheimnis zu wahren;
    Ach, den Lippen entquillt Fülle des Herzens so leicht!
Keiner Freundin darf ichs vertraun: sie möchte mich schelten;
    Keinem Freunde: vielleicht brächte der Freund mir Gefahr.
Mein Entzücken dem Hain, dem schallenden Felsen zu sagen,
    Bin ich endlich nicht jung, bin ich nicht einsam genug.
Dir, Hexameter, dir, Pentameter, sei es vertrauet,
    Wie sie des Tags mich erfreut, wie sie des Nachts mich
        beglückt.   570
Sie, von vielen Männern gesucht, vermeidet die Schlingen,
    Die ihr der Kühnere frech, heimlich der Listige legt;
Klug und zierlich schlüpft sie vorbei und kennet die Wege,
    Wo sie der Liebste gewiß lauschend begierig empfängt.
Zaudre, Luna, sie kommt! damit sie der Nachbar nicht sehe;
    Rausche, Lüftchen, im Laub! niemand vernehme den Tritt.
Und ihr, wachset und blüht, geliebte Lieder, und wieget
    Euch im leisesten Hauch lauer und liebender Luft,
Und entdeckt den Quiriten, wie jene Rohre geschwätzig,
    Eines glücklichen Paars schönes Geheimnis zuletzt.   580

XXIII

Strength, and a bold and liberal nature, are virtues a man needs;
  And even more, he must know how to keep things to himself.   550
Goddess Discretion! defeater of cities and ruler of peoples!
  Dear protectress, my sure guide through the perils of life,
See what a pass I am in! My lips are sealed, but the laughing
  Muse and the Love-god, that rogue, tempt me and loosen my
    tongue.
Ah, how hard it becomes to cover up royal disgraces!
  Midas* needs more than a crown, more than a Phrygian cap
If he would hide his ass-ears. His closest servant has seen them,
  And a secret so dire heavily weighs on his mind.
He'd like to bury it deep in the earth, for that would relieve him;
  But such secrets as this even the earth will not keep.   560
Reeds spring up, and when the wind blows they rustle and
    murmur:
  'Midas, Midas the king, Midas has long pointed ears!'
Now it is growing harder for me to keep a sweet secret;
  Ah, when the heart is so full, easily lips overflow!
Which of my friends can I tell? Not a woman, for she might
    reproach me;
  Not a man either, for he might be a rival to fear.
And to confide my joy to the grove, to the rocks and their
    echoes—
  That is for lonesome youth, that will not do at my age.
Listen, hexameter, listen, pentameter: you, then, shall hear it—
  How she delights me by day, how she enchants me by night!   570
Many men seek her favours and try to ensnare her, the bold ones
  Crudely, the cunning ones more subtly; but all she outwits.
Prudently, gracefully, she slips by, for she knows where her lover
  Ardently listens and waits, knows hidden ways to his arms.
Moonlight, oh hesitate now—she is coming: no neighbour must
    see her!
  Rustle the leaves, little breeze; no one must hear her approach!
And you, oh my beloved songs, may you blossom and flourish,
  Swaying in love's warm winds, rocked by their gentlest breath;
Chatter as those reeds did, and at last tell Rome all about us:
  Tell of two lovers whose glad secret is secret no more.   580

XXIV
[EPILOG]

Hinten im Winkel des Gartens, da stand ich, der letzte der Götter,
    Rohgebildet, und schlimm hatte die Zeit mich verletzt.
Kürbisranken schmiegten sich auf am veralteten Stamme,
    Und schon krachte das Glied unter den Lasten der Frucht.
Dürres Gereisig neben mir an, dem Winter gewidmet,
    Den ich hasse, denn er schickt mir die Raben aufs Haupt,
Schändlich mich zu besudeln; der Sommer sendet die Knechte,
    Die, sich entladende, frech zeigen das rohe Gesäß.
Unflat oben und unten! ich mußte fürchten ein Unflat
    Selber zu werden, ein Schwamm, faules verlorenes Holz. 590
Nun, durch deine Bemühung, o! redlicher Künstler, gewinn ich
    Unter Göttern den Platz, der mir und andern gebührt.
Wer hat Jupiters Thron, den schlechterworbnen, befestigt?
    Farb und Elfenbein, Marmor und Erz und Gedicht.
Gern erblicken mich nun verständige Männer, und denken
    Mag sich jeder so gern, wie es der Künstler gedacht.
Nicht das Mädchen entsetzt sich vor mir, und nicht die Matrone,
    Häßlich bin ich nicht mehr, bin ungeheuer nur stark.
Dafür soll dir denn auch halbfußlang die prächtige Rute
    Strotzen vom Mittel herauf, wenn es die Liebste gebeut, 600
Soll das Glied nicht ermüden, als bis ihr die Dutzend Figuren
    Durchgenossen, wie sie künstlich Philänis erfand.

XXIV*
[EPILOGUE]

Once in the garden's far corner I stood, the last and the least god,
    Coarsely carved, and ill-used by the rude ravage of time.
Gourd-plant tendrils entwined my perishing trunk, and already
    My poor member had cracked under the weight of the fruit.
Broken branches lay by me, dry withered twigs for the winter;
    How I hate winter! that's when ravens, detestable birds,
Drop all their filth on my head; and in summer the insolent gardeners
    Squat here relieving themselves, showing their ugly backsides.
Shit from upstairs and downstairs! I feared even I would be turning
    Into a spongy old turd, nothing but rotten waste wood.   590
Now, thanks to your good work, honest craftsman, I have been granted
    My due place among gods, fitting for me and for all.
What has kept Jove on his ill-gotten throne, and established it soundly?
    Colour and ivory, bronze, marble and poetry's art.
Now I'm a sight for intelligent men, they all like to imagine
    They themselves are as well made as the artist made me.
Girls are no longer shocked when they see me, and neither are matrons,
    For I'm not hideous now, I'm just enormously strong.
Therefore I bless your magnificent central rod, may it always
    Stand up half a foot tall at your beloved's behest.   600
May your member not tire, until you have both done the dozen
    Figures Philaenis* describes, finished the dance of your joy.

Aus den
VENEZIANISCHEN EPIGRAMMEN

From the
VENETIAN EPIGRAMS

1

Sarkophagen und Urnen verzierte der Heide mit Leben:
   Faunen tanzen umher, mit der Bacchantinnen Chor
Machen sie bunte Reihe; der ziegengefüßete Pausback
   Zwingt den heiseren Ton wild aus dem schmetternden Horn.
Zymbeln, Trommeln erklingen; wir sehen und hören den Marmor.
   Flatternde Vögel! wie schmeckt herrlich dem Schnabel die
     Frucht!
Euch verscheuchet kein Lärm, noch weniger scheucht er den
     Amor,
   Der in dem bunten Gewühl erst sich der Fackel erfreut.
So überwältiget Fülle den Tod; und die Asche da drinnen
   Scheint, im stillen Bezirk, noch sich des Lebens zu freun.   10
So umgebe denn spät den Sarkophagen des Dichters
   Diese Rolle, von ihm reichlich mit Leben geschmückt.

2

Glänzen sah ich das Meer und blinken die liebliche Welle,
   Frisch mit günstigem Wind zogen die Segel dahin.
Keine Sehnsucht fühlte mein Herz; es wendete rückwärts,
   Nach dem Schnee des Gebirgs, bald sich der schmachtende
     Blick.
Südwärts liegen der Schätze wie viel! Doch einer im Norden
   Zieht, ein großer Magnet, unwiderstehlich zurück.

1

Pagan burial-urns and sarcophagi, how they adorned them
  With so much life! How they leap, Bacchants in chorus and
    fauns,
Alternating their dance, as the goatfooted satyr* with cheeks
    puffed
  Forces the harsh wild notes out of his loud braying horn!
Cymbals and drums resound; we are seeing and hearing the
    marble.
  How the birds flutter, their beaks savouring wonderful fruit!
No noise startles them now, still less will the Love-god be startled
  In this fine medley of joy where he can brandish his flame.
Thus mortality yields to abundance; the ashes within still
  Seem, in this quiet place, to be alive and astir.   10
Thus, one day, may a poet's sarcophagus wear the adornment
  Of this scroll of his words, filled with the beauty of life.

2

Now in the shine of the sea, on the fair waves glittering brightly,
  Ships in full sail I saw, chased by the favouring breeze;
But my heart felt no longing, my eyes soon turned with such
    hunger
  Back to the mountains and snow, back to where lately I'd been.
There in the south what treasures await me! But one, a great
    loadstone,
  With irresistible power still draws me northwards* again.

3

Das ist Italien, das ich verließ. Noch stäuben die Wege,
    Noch ist der Fremde geprellt, stell er sich, wie er auch will.   20
Deutsche Redlichkeit suchst du in allen Winkeln vergebens;
    Leben und Weben ist hier, aber nicht Ordnung und Zucht;
Jeder sorgt nur für sich, mißtrauet dem andern, ist eitel,
    Und die Meister des Staats sorgen nur wieder für sich.
Schön ist das Land; doch ach! Faustinen find ich nicht wieder.
    Das ist Italien nicht mehr, das ich mit Schmerzen verließ.

4

Wundern kann es mich nicht, daß Menschen die Hunde so lieben:
    Denn ein erbärmlicher Schuft ist, wie der Mensch, so der Hund.

5

Ist denn so groß das Geheimniß, was Gott und der Mensch und
    die Welt sei?
    Nein! Doch niemand mags gern hören;* da bleibt es geheim.   30

3

This is the country I left, this is Italy! Roads still all dusty;
  Still full of tourists, who try not to be swindled but fail.
Search high and low here for German honesty, and you'll not find
    it.
  Plentiful life, to be sure; order and discipline, none!
It's every man for himself here; mistrustful they are, and conceited.
  As for the lords of the State, they too just feather their nests.
It's a fine land; but alas, where now is my lovely Faustina?
  Where is the Italy now I was grief-stricken to leave?

4

I'm not surprised that dogs are beloved companions of mankind:
  Dog and man are alike, each a contemptible cur.*

5

Is it so great, the great secret, what God and mankind and the
    world are?
  No! But we don't want to know; so we have left it unsaid.

6

Diese Gondel vergleich ich der sanft einschaukelnden Wiege,
  Und das Kästchen darauf scheint ein geräumiger Sarg.
Recht so! Zwischen der Wieg und dem Sarg wir schwanken und
    schweben
  Auf dem großen Kanal sorglos durchs Leben dahin.

7

Gleich den Winken des Mädchens, des eilenden, welches
    verstohlen
  Im Vorbeigehn nur freundlich mir streifet den Arm,
So vergönnt, ihr Musen, dem Reisenden kleine Gedichte:
  O, behaltet dem Freund größere Gunst noch bevor!

8

In dem engsten der Gäßchen — es drängte sich kaum durch die
    Mauern —
  Saß mir ein Mädchen im Weg, als ich Venedig durchlief.
Sie war reizend, der Ort, ich ließ mich Fremder verführen;
  Ach, ein weiter Kanal that sich dem Forschenden auf.
Hättest du Mädchen wie deine Kanäle, Venedig, und Fötzchen
  Wie die Gäßchen in dir, wärst du die herrlichste Stadt.

40

6

I'd say this gondola's just like a cradle, it rocks me so gently,
    And its cabin on top's like a big coffin. Indeed!
Thus from cradle to grave through our life we are rocking and
       floating
    As on a Grand Canal, carefree betwixt and between.

7

Like a girl's surreptitious gesture, when hurrying past me
    She with no more than a touch lightly caresses my arm:
Grant that the traveller now, dear Muses, may write little poems,
    And may your friend still have hope of greater favour to come.

8

There was a street here in Venice, so narrow I scarcely could
       push my
    Way through it, and with a girl sitting there blocking my path.   40
But she was charming, and—well, the place puts its spell on a
       stranger;
    So I explore . . . But what's this, what a canal I'm in now!
Venice, if all your canals were girls, and if only their cunts were
    Like your alleyways—what city could vie with you then!

9

Gib mir statt 'Der Schwanz' ein ander Wort, o Priapus,
  Denn ich Deutscher, ich bin übel als Dichter geplagt.
Griechisch nennt ich dich φαλλός, das klänge doch prächtig den
    Ohren,
  Und lateinisch ist auch *mentula* leidlich ein Wort.
Mentula käme von *mens*, der Schwanz ist etwas von hinten,
  Und nach hinten war mir niemals ein froher Genuß.   50

10

Knaben liebt ich wohl auch, doch lieber sind mir die Mädchen:
  Hab ich als Mädchen sie satt, dient sie als Knabe mir noch.

11

Längst schon hätt ich euch gern von jenen Tierchen gesprochen,
  Die so zierlich und schnell fahren dahin und daher.
Schlängelchen scheinen sie gleich, doch viergefüßet; sie laufen,
    Kriechen und schleichen, und leicht schleppen die
      Schwänzchen sie nach.
Seht, hier sind sie! und hier! Nun sind sie verschwunden! Wo
    sind sie?
  Welche Ritze, welch Kraut nahm die entfliehenden auf?
Wollt ihr mirs künftig erlauben, so nenn ich die Tierchen
    Lacerten;
  Denn ich brauche sie noch oft als gefälliges Bild.   60

9

Give me, Priapus, another name for it! *Schwanz* is the German
　　Word, devil take it, for 'tail'; what's a poor poet to do?
Φαλλός I'd call it in Greek, that would be very fine and
　　　high-sounding;
　　And a Roman would say *mentula*;* that too would serve;
It's from *mens*, I suppose, meaning 'mind'. But a *tail*'s on one's
　　　backside:
　　And backsidewise—well, that never was my kind of fun.   50

10

Well, I suppose I've loved boys* as well; but girls are much better.
　　When she's lost charm as a girl, give her a turn as a boy.

11

I've been meaning to tell you about those neat little creatures,
　　How they all scuttle so fast, how they all dart to and fro.
They are like tiny snakes, but four-footed; look at them running,
　　Creeping and crawling! Their tails follow them, as you can see.
Look, here are some! and some here! They've vanished now.
　　　Where have they got to?
　　Under what bush have they fled, into what crack in the ground?
From now on, by your leave, I shall call these creatures *lacertae*;*
　　For to add charm to my verse, they are the image I need.   60

12

Wer Lacerten gesehn, der kann sich die zierlichen Mädchen
   Denken, die über den Platz fahren dahin und daher.
Schnell und beweglich sind sie, und gleiten, stehen und schwatzen,
   Und es rauscht das Gewand hinter den eilenden drein.
Sieh, hier ist sie! und hier! Verlierst du sie einmal, so suchst du
   Sie vergebens; so bald kommt sie nicht wieder hervor.
Wenn du aber die Winkel nicht scheust, nicht Gäßchen und
      Treppchen,
   Folg ihr, wie sie dich lockt, in die Spelunke hinein!

13

Was Spelunke nun sei, verlangt ihr zu wissen? Da wird ja
   Fast zum Lexikon dies epigrammatische Buch.   70
Dunkele Häuser sinds in engen Gäßchen; zum Kaffee
   Führt dich die Schöne, und sie zeigt sich geschäftig, nicht du.

12

If you know what *lacertae* are like, you'll recognize all those
  Charming young girls that one sees darting about on the square.
They're very agile and quick, they slink and they stand and they
      chatter,
  And each one hurries by, whisking her skirt like a tail.
Look, here she is! and now here! Don't lose her, or you'll be
      searching
  High and low till she comes out of her hiding again.
But if you don't mind dubious dives, little alleys and stairways,
  Follow her beckoning hand: here's her *spelunca*!* Come in!

13

'What's a *spelunca*?' I hear you ask, 'please explain!' (Goodness
      me, this
  Epigrammatical book's almost a lexicon now.)   70
It's a dark little den in a narrow alley: the lady
  Offers you coffee—which means: she does the work and not you.

14

Seid ihr ein Fremder, mein Herr? bewohnt ihr Venedig? so
    fragten
  Zwei Lacerten, die mich in die Spelunke gelockt.
Ratet! — Ihr seid ein Franzos! ein Napolitaner! Sie schwatzten
  Hin und wieder und schnell schlürften sie Kaffee hinein.
Tun wir etwas! sagte die Schönste, sie setzte die Tasse
  Nieder, ich fühlte sogleich ihre geschäftige Hand.
Sacht ergriff ich und hielte sie fest; da streckte die zweite
  Zierliche Fingerchen aus, und ich verwehrt es auch ihr.   80
Ach, es ist ein Fremder! so riefen sie beide; sie scherzten,
  Baten Geschenke sich aus, die ich doch sparsam verlieh.
Drauf bezeichneten sie mir die entferntere Wohnung
  Und zu dem wärmeren Spiel spätere Stunden der Nacht.
Kannten diese Geschöpfe sogleich den Fremden am Weigern,
  O, so wißt ihr, warum blaß der Venetier schleicht.

15

'Kaffee wollen wir trinken, mein Fremder!' — da meint sie
    branlieren;
  Hab ich doch, Freunde, mit Recht immer den Kaffee gehaßt.

14

'Are you a foreigner, sir?' two *lacertae* in their *spelunca*
  Asked when they'd lured me inside, 'or a Venetian perhaps?'
'Guess!' 'I think you're a Frenchman!' 'I think you're from
    Naples!' They chattered
  Idly, and hurriedly swilled coffee in cup after cup.
'Come on, let's do something!' said the best-looking one, putting
    her cup down.
  And sure enough, there it was, her little rummaging hand.
Gently I caught it in mine and restrained it. The second of them
    then
  Brought busy fingers to bear; I put a stop to that too.   80
'Oh dear,' they both exclaimed, 'he's a foreigner!' So they cajoled
    me;
  'Give us a present!' they teased, but my largess was not great.
Then I was told of a house further off, where some more
    entertainment,
  Later that night, could be had, of a more intimate kind.
Well! If these creatures at once knew a foreigner by his reluctance,
  That's why the men of this town wander so wanly about.

15

'Stranger-man, come, let's drink coffee!' she says, and she means
    'let me wank you'.
  So much for coffee, my friends; I've always hated the stuff.

16

'Wär ich ein häusliches Weib, und hätte, was ich bedürfte,
  Treu sein wollt ich und froh, herzen und küssen den Mann.'   90
So sang, unter andern gemeinen Liedern, ein Dirnchen
  Mir in Venedig, und nie hört ich ein frömmer Gebet.

17

Lange sucht ich ein Weib mir; ich suchte, da fand ich nur Dirnen;
  Endlich erhascht ich dich mir, Dirnchen; da fand ich ein Weib!

18

Welch ein Mädchen ich wünsche zu haben? ihr fragt mich. Ich
    hab sie,
  Wie ich sie wünsche. Das heißt, dünkt mich, mit wenigem viel.
An dem Meere ging ich, und suchte mir Muscheln. In einer
  Fand ich ein Perlchen; es bleibt nun mir am Herzen verwahrt.

16

'If I'd the husband I need, and if I kept house for him, I'd be
   Happy and faithful and true, hug him and kiss him all day.'   90
That was the song, among others more coarse, of a little Venetian
   Whore; and so pious a prayer never I heard in my life.

17

In my long search for a wife, I kept picking up whores; in the
   end I
   Caught you, dear little whore: now I have found me a wife!

18

What kind of girl do I long for, you ask me? I have one already
   Who is all that I want; and for a little, that's much.
Down by the sea I was walking and looking for shells, and in one
   shell
   There was a pearl of great price: now it lives close to my heart.

19

Wundern kann es mich nicht, daß unser Herr Christus mit Dirnen
    Gern und mit Sündern gelebt, gehts mir doch eben auch so.   100

20

Wie dem hohen Apostel ein Tuch voll Tiere gezeigt ward,
    Rein und unrein, zeigt, Lieber, das Büchlein sich dir.

21

Wie von der künstlichsten Hand geschnitzt das liebe Figürchen,
    Weich und ohne Gebein, wie die Molluska nur schwimmt!
Alles ist Glied, und alles Gelenk, und alles gefällig,
    Alles nach Maßen gebaut, alles nach Willkür bewegt.
Menschen hab ich gekannt und Tiere, so Vögel als Fische,
    Manches besondre Gewürm, Wunder der großen Natur;
Und doch staun ich dich an, Bettine, liebliches Wunder,
    Die du alles zugleich bist, und ein Engel dazu.   110

19

I'm not surprised that our Lord Jesus Christ liked consorting with
    sinners
    And with whores; after all, that's just what I fancy too.   100

20

As the Apostle* was shown a mixed bundle of beasts in his vision,
    So shall my book, dear friend, offer you clean and unclean.

21

Dear little shape that might have been carved by the hand of an
    artist!
    Supple and boneless she seems, molluscoid, floating at ease.
All of her body is limbs, all joints, and all of it pleasing;
    All of it measured and made, all of it wilful and free.
Many the human and animal creatures, the birds and the fishes,
    Curious creeping things, wonders of nature I've known:
Yet you amaze me still, Bettina,* sweet natural wonder!
    For you are all these at once, and a dear angel as well.   110

22

Wende die Füßchen zum Himmel nur ohne Sorge! Wir strecken
  Arme betend empor; aber nicht schuldlos, wie du.

23

Alles seh ich so gerne von dir; doch seh ich am liebsten,
  Wenn der Vater behend über dich selber dich wirft,
Du dich im Schwung überschlägst und, nach dem tödlichen
    Sprunge,
  Wieder stehest und läufst, eben ob nichts wär geschehn.

24

Auszuspannen befiehlt der Vater die zierlichen Schenkel;
  Kindisch der liebliche Teil sinkt auf den Teppich herab.
Ach, wer einst zuerst dich liebet, er findet die Blüte
  Schon verschwunden, sie nahm frühe das Handwerk hinweg.   120

22

Turn your toes up to heaven, my dear, and don't worry! We reach
   up
   Heavenwards too with our hands, but not so innocently.

23

Watching all that you do is so pleasant; but what I enjoy most
   Is when your father's quick hands hurl you up over yourself
Into a somersault, and you drop down as if nothing had happened,
   Standing and running again, after this perilous leap.

24

Now, at your father's command, your delicate thighs are extended,
   And that most charming of parts, childlike, is touching the
      ground.
One day, alas, the first of your lovers will find that your maiden
   Flower* has vanished: your trade snatched it away long ago.   120

25

Was ich am meisten besorge: Bettine wird immer geschickter,
    Immer beweglicher wird jegliches Gliedchen an ihr;
Endlich bringt sie das Züngelchen noch ins zierliche Fötzchen,
    Spielt mit dem artigen selbst, achtet die Männer nicht viel.

26

So verwirret mit dumpf willkürlich verwebten Gestalten,
    Höllisch und trübe gesinnt, Breughel den schwankenden Blick;
So zerrüttet auch Dürer mit apokalyptischen Bildern,
    Menschen und Grillen zugleich, unser gesundes Gehirn;
So erreget ein Dichter, von Sphinxen, Sirenen, Centauren
    Singend, mit Macht Neugier in dem verwunderten Ohr;   130
So beweget ein Traum den Sorglichen, wenn er zu greifen,
    Vorwärts glaubet zu gehn, alles veränderlich schwebt:
So verwirrt uns Bettine, die holden Glieder verwechselnd,
    Doch erfreut sie uns gleich, wenn sie die Sohlen betritt.

25

My chief anxiety is that Bettina gets more and more skilful:
   Each of her soft little limbs, suppler and suppler it grows.
She'll end up with her delicate tongue in her delicate pussy,
   Learning to play with herself: what will her lovers do then?

26

This is how Bruegel, capriciously, darkly, with forms interwoven,
   In an inferno of gloom, troubles and puzzles our gaze;
This is how Dürer* subverts our brains when they're perfectly
      normal,
   With men and monsters, with weird apocalyptical shapes;
This is how poets who sing about sphinxes and sirens and
      centaurs
   Rule us with curious thoughts, tease and astonish our ears;   130
This is how dreams afflict anxious sleepers, who seem to walk
      forwards,
   Seem to be clutching at things, things all in flux and afloat;
This is how sweet Bettina confuses her limbs to confound us;
   But then she gladdens our hearts, landing once more on her
      feet.

27

'Welch ein Wahnsinn ergriff dich Müßigen? Hältst du nicht inne?
  Wird dies Mädchen ein Buch? Stimme was Klügeres an!'
Wartet, ich singe die Könige bald, die Großen der Erde,
  Wenn ich ihr Handwerk einst besser begreife wie jetzt.
Doch Bettinen sing ich indes: denn Gaukler und Dichter
  Sind gar nahe verwandt, suchen und finden sich gern.   140

28

Heraus mit dem Teile des Herrn! heraus mit dem Teile des
      Gottes!
  Rief ein unglücklich Geschöpf, blind vor hysterischer Wut,
Als, die heiligen Reste Gründonnerstag Abends zu zeigen,
  In Sankt Markus ein Schelm über der Bühne sich wies.
Armes Mädchen, was soll dir ein Teil des gekreuzigten Gottes?
  Rufe den heilsamern Teil jenes von Lampsacus her.

27

'You must be mad, or have too much time! Why don't you just
    stop it?
    This girl's becoming a book! Find some more sensible theme.'
All in good time; one day I shall sing about princes and great folk,
    When I have studied their trade, and know it better than now.
Meanwhile, I shall sing of Bettina; for jugglers and poets
    Like to make friends and to keep company; they are close kin.   140

28

'Show us the parts of the Lord!' shrieked, blind with hysterical
    frenzy,
    An unfortunate girl: 'Show us the parts of our god!'
It was the evening of Holy Thursday, a priest was displaying
    (So the old charlatan claimed) relics of Christ in St Mark's.
Poor soul! Why do you cry out like this for the crucified god's
    parts?
    Cry for Priapus! That god's parts are the medicine you need.*

29

Vieles kann ich ertragen. Die meisten beschwerlichen Dinge
　　Duld ich mit ruhigem Mut, wie es ein Gott mir gebeut.
Wenige sind mir jedoch wie Gift und Schlange zuwider,
　　Viere: Rauch des Tabaks, Wanzen und Knoblauch und Christ.* 150

30

Böcke, zur Linken mit euch! so ordnet künftig der Richter,
　　Und ihr Schäfchen, ihr sollt ruhig zur Rechten mir stehn!
Wohl! Doch eines ist noch von ihm zu hoffen; dann sagt er:
　　Seid, Vernünftige, mir grad gegenüber gestellt!

31

Sauber hast du dein Volk erlöst durch Wunder und Leiden,
　　Nazarener! Wohin soll es, dein Häufchen, wohin?
Leben sollen sie doch und Kinder zeugen doch christlich,
　　Leider dem früheren Reiz dienet die schädliche Hand.
Will der Jüngling dem Übel entgehn, sich selbst nicht verderben,
　　Bringet Lais ihm nur brennende Qualen für Lust.   160
Komm noch einmal herab, du Gott der Schöpfung, und leide,
　　Komm, erlöse dein Volk von dem gedoppelten Weh!
Tu ein Wunder und reinge die Quellen der Freud und des
　　　Lebens —
　　Paulus will ich dir sein, Stephanus, wie dus gebeutst.

29

Many things I can endure; they are burdensome, yet for the most
    part
  Patiently I can submit, bowing to heaven's decree.
But there are just four things, like wormwood and gall I abhor
    them:
  Reeking tobacco-smoke, bugs, garlic, and Christ on the cross.   150

30

'Goats, go and stand on my left!' so the Judge at the last day will
    order.
  'And as for you, little sheep, come to my right, if you please.'
Excellent! But let us hope he will make one further announcement:
  'Now, you men of good sense, face me, and stand straight
    ahead!'

31

Wonders indeed you have done for your people, oh Nazarene!
    Now by
  Suffering they are redeemed; but whither now, little flock?
For they must still live, still beget children, yet do so like
    Christians—
  And the injurious hand serves their old promptings too well.
How's a poor youth to escape from such vice and avoid his own
    ruin?
  Lais* will do him no good, she'll inflict pleasures that burn.   160
Come down again, oh God of creation, and suffer again here!
  Come, bring your people a new cure for this double-edged woe!
Cleanse the sources of joy and of life by some miracle! I'll be
  Your St Paul in that cause, Stephen* as well if you like.

32

Willst du die Freuden* der Liebe mit reinem Gefühle genießen,
  O! so laß Frechheit und Ernst ferne vom Herzen dir sein;
Jene will Amorn verjagen, und dieser gedenkt ihn zu fesseln.
  Siehe, da lächelt der Gott beiden das Gegenteil zu.

33

O, wie achtet ich sonst auf alle Zeiten des Jahres,
  Grüßte den kommenden Lenz, sehnte dem Herbste mich nach!   170
Aber nun ist nicht Sommer noch Winter, seit mich Beglückten
  Amors Fittich bedeckt, ewiger Frühling umschwebt.

34

Ob erfüllt sei, was Moses und was die Propheten gesprochen,
  An dem heiligen Christ, Freunde, das weiß ich nicht recht.
Aber das weiß ich: erfüllt sind Wünsche, Sehnsucht und Träume,
  Wenn das liebliche Kind süß mir am Busen entschläft.

32

If you would single-heartedly taste the pleasure of love, oh
   Shun the too cynical, shun also the earnest approach.
For the first tries to drive Love away, and the second to bind him:
   But the god's mischievous smile shows him contrary to both.

33

Oh, how intently I used to observe all the year's four seasons,
   Greeting the springtime's approach, longing for autumn to
   come!
Now I live neither in summer nor winter, now that the
   Love-god's
   Wings caress me with joy, with a perpetual spring.

170

34

Whether the words of the prophets and Moses have come to
   fulfilment
   With Christ's Nativity—well, that, my dear friends, I don't
   know.
But I do know all my dreams are fulfilled, all my wishes and
   longings,
   When my sweet darling is here, and falls asleep in my arms.

35

Welche Hoffnung ich habe? Nur eine, die heut mich beschäftigt:
  Morgen mein Liebchen zu sehn, das ich acht Tage nicht sah.

36

Alles, was ihr wollt, ich bin euch wie immer gewärtig.
  Freunde, doch leider: allein schlafen, ich halt es nicht aus.   180

37

Welch ein lustiges Spiel! Es windet am Faden die Scheibe,
  Die von der Hand entfloh, eilig sich wieder herauf!
Seht, so schein ich mein Herz bald dieser Schönen, bald jener
  Zuzuwerfen; doch gleich kehrt es im Fluge zurück.

35

How can I have any hope, you ask me?—Just one, for tomorrow:
  To see my sweetheart! I've not been with her now for a week.

36

Ask me what favour you will, my dear friends, I'll be glad to
    oblige you:
  But go to bed by myself?—That, by your leave, I'll not bear! 180

37

What an agreeable toy! A disc on a string,* I unwind it,
  Casting it out of my hand, and it rewinds in a trice.
That's how I seem to be casting my heart at this and that beauty:
  But it is never long gone, bounces straight back, as you see.

38

Weit und schön ist die Welt; doch o wie dank ich dem Himmel,
  Daß Dein Gärtchen, beschränkt, zierlich, mein eigen gehört!
Bringet mich wieder nach Hause! Was hat ein Gärtner zu reisen?
  Ehre bringts ihm und Glück, wenn er sein Gärtchen versorgt.

39

Ach, mein Hals ist ein wenig geschwollen! so sagte die Beste
  Ängstlich. — Stille, mein Kind! still! und vernehme das Wort: 190
Dich hat die Hand der Venus berührt; sie deutet dir leise,
  Daß sie das Körperchen bald, ach! unaufhaltsam verstellt.
Bald verdirbt sie die schlanke Gestalt, die zierlichen Brüstchen.
  Alles schwillt nun; es paßt nirgends das neuste Gewand.
Sei nur ruhig! es deutet die fallende Blüte dem Gärtner,
  Daß die liebliche Frucht schwellend im Herbste gedeiht.

38

Wide is the world and beautiful, but I am thankful to heaven
    That *your* garden is small, dainty, and my very own!
Take me back home again! Why should a gardener travel?
        Sufficient
    Honour and joy will be his from his own husbandry here.

39

'Oh dear, my neck is all swollen!' she said rather anxiously.
        Sweetheart,
    Hush, and listen to me! Venus has touched you, my child: 190
This is a gentle message from her, that presently she will
    Visit your body, alas, with irresistible change.
She will distort your slender figure, your delicate breasts will
    Swell with the rest of you, no dresses will fit any more.
Don't let it trouble you; for any gardener knows, when the
        blossoms
    Fall, the delectable fruit swells towards harvesting-time.

40

Wonniglich ists, die Geliebte verlangend im Arme zu halten,
  Wenn ihr klopfendes Herz Liebe zuerst dir gesteht.
Wonniglicher, das Pochen des Neulebendigen fühlen,
  Das in dem lieblichen Schoß immer sich nährend bewegt.   200
Schon versucht es die Sprünge der raschen Jugend; es klopfet
  Ungeduldig schon an, sehnt sich nach himmlischem Licht.
Harre noch wenige Tage! Auf allen Pfaden des Lebens
  Führen die Horen dich streng, wie es das Schicksal gebeut.
Widerfahre dir, was dir auch will, du wachsender Liebling —
  Liebe bildete dich; werde dir Liebe zu teil!

41

Und so tändelt ich mir, von allen Freuden geschieden,
  In der Neptunischen Stadt Tage wie Stunden hinweg.
Alles, was ich erfuhr, ich würzt es mit süßer Erinnrung,
  Würzt es mit Hoffnung; sie sind lieblichste Würzen der Welt.   210

40

It is such joy to hug my beloved so close, to desire her,
    And in her heartbeat to hear her first confession of love:
Joy still greater to feel life coming, another life pulsing
    As it moves, as it thrives, in her dear nourishing womb!   200
Now already it leaps up boldly, in youthful impatience
    Knocking and pushing its way, longing for heavenly light.
Wait for a few days longer! The Hours* must strictly conduct you
    On all the paths of your life, leading as Fate has decreed.
Let it decree for you what it will, little growing-up darling—
    For you were fashioned by love; may you know love in your turn!

41

Parted from all my joy,* in this Neptunian city,*
    Thus I trifled the days, trifled the hours away.
All I experienced here has been seasoned with sweet recollection
    And sweet hope; there is no seasoning finer than these.   210

DAS TAGEBUCH

THE DIARY*

—aliam tenui, sed iam quum gaudia adirem,
Admonuit dominae deseruitque Venus.*

I

Wir hörens oft und glaubens wohl am Ende:
Das Menschenherz sei ewig unergründlich,
Und wie man auch sich hin und wider wende,
So sei der Christe wie der Heide sündlich.
Das Beste bleibt, wir geben uns die Hände
Und nehmens mit der Lehre nicht empfindlich;
Denn zeigt sich auch ein Dämon, uns versuchend,
So waltet was, gerettet ist die Tugend.

II

Von meiner Trauten lange Zeit entfernet,
Wies öfters geht, nach irdischem Gewinne,   10
Und was ich auch gewonnen und gelernet,
So hatt ich doch nur immer Sie im Sinne;
Und wie zu Nacht der Himmel erst sich sternet,
Erinnrung uns umleuchtet ferner Minne:
So ward im Federzug des Tags Ereignis
Mit süßen Worten Ihr ein freundlich Gleichnis.

III

Ich eilte nun zurück. Zerbrochen sollte
Mein Wagen mich noch eine Nacht verspäten;
Schon dacht ich mich, wie ich zu Hause rollte,
Allein da war Geduld und Werk vonnöten.   20
Und wie ich auch mit Schmied und Wagner tollte,
Sie hämmerten, verschmähten viel zu reden.
Ein jedes Handwerk hat nun seine Schnurren.
Was blieb mir nun? Zu weilen und zu murren.

I

The saying goes—it's true enough, no doubt—
That man's heart is for ever fathomless:
That Christians, though they turn and turn about,
Are sinners still, like pagans. Let's confess
As much, and all shake hands! We carry out
What Virtue bids us, only rather less;
Why fret? For when by some wild imp we're tempted
Another force prevails, and sin's preempted.

II

It happened, as so often, travelling
For worldly profit, I'd been some time parted   10
From my true love; and many a useful thing
I'd done and learnt—but always, faithful-hearted,
Thinking of her. At night's first glittering
Of stars, remembered love's bright fire is started:
So too, I'd pen the doings of my day
In sweet words for my darling far away.

III

Now, hurrying back to her, misfortune struck
My homeward course: a broken wheel delayed me.
So soon I'd have been there! Now I was stuck.
O workmanship, what a droll trick you'd played me!   20
I cursed the smith, the wainwright and my luck;
They hammered on, and scant reply they made me.
I wait, they ply their mystery. What a crew!
But stay the night was all that I could do.

IV

So stand ich nun! Der Stern des nächsten Schildes
Berief mich hin, die Wohnung schien erträglich.
Ein Mädchen kam, des seltensten Gebildes,
Das Licht erleuchtend. Mir ward gleich behäglich.
Hausflur und Treppe sah ich als ein Mildes,
Die Zimmerchen erfreuten mich unsäglich. 30
Den sündgen Menschen, der im Freien schwebet —
Die Schönheit spinnt, sie ists die ihn umwebet.

V

Nun setzt ich mich zu meiner Tasch und Briefen
Und meines Tagebuchs Genauigkeiten,
Um so wie sonst, wenn alle Menschen schliefen,
Mir und der Trauten Freude zu bereiten;
Doch weiß ich nicht, die Tintenworte liefen
Nicht so wie sonst in alle Kleinigkeiten:
Das Mädchen kam, des Abendessens Bürde
Verteilte sie gewandt mit Gruß und Würde. 40

VI

Sie geht und kommt; ich spreche, sie erwidert.
Mit jedem Wort erscheint sie mir geschmückter.
Und wie sie leicht mir nun das Huhn zergliedert,
Bewegend Hand und Arm, geschickt, geschickter —
Was auch das tolle Zeug in uns befiedert,
Genug, ich bin verworrner, bin verrückter,
Den Stuhl umwerfend spring ich auf und fasse
Das schöne Kind; sie lispelt: Lasse, lasse!

IV

So there I stood. The nearest hostelry
Was called 'The Star'; it looked a decent place.
A girl appeared—a shapely rarity—
With lamp and light; my spirits rose apace.
The hallway and the stairs delighted me,
The little rooms seemed full of charm and grace.   30
When sinful mortals wander far from home,
Beauty's fine web may catch them as they roam.

V

So I sat down to my portfolio,
My letters, and my diary's exact
Reports: nocturnal words, which I would show
As always to my dearest. Yet they lacked
Somehow tonight their usual easy flow;
The ink ran sluggish round each trifling fact.
The girl brought in my supper, greeted me
And laid it out with skill and dignity.   40

VI

She comes and goes, and as we talk I'm stricken
With growing admiration for her charm.
I watch how cleverly she carves my chicken
With quick, deft movements of her hand and arm:
How my mad feathers sprout, my pulses quicken!
In short, my head's confused, my heart is warm,
And up I jump, knock the chair over, seize
The pretty creature—but she whispers: 'Please,

VII

Die Muhme drunten lauscht, ein alter Drache,
Sie zählt bedächtig des Geschäfts Minute;   50
Sie denkt sich unten, was ich oben mache,
Bei jedem Zögern schwenkt sie frisch die Rute.
Doch schließe deine Türe nicht und wache,
So kommt die Mitternacht uns wohl zu Gute.
Rasch meinem Arm entwindet sie die Glieder,
Und eilet fort und kommt nur dienend wieder;

VIII

Doch blickend auch! so daß aus jedem Blicke
Sich himmlisches Versprechen mir entfaltet.
Den stillen Seufzer drängt sie nicht zurücke,
Der ihren Busen herrlicher gestaltet.   60
Ich sehe, daß am Ohr, um Hals und Gnicke
Der flüchtgen Röte Liebesblüte waltet,
Und da sie nichts zu leisten weiter findet,
Geht sie und zögert, sieht sich um, verschwindet.

IX

Der Mitternacht gehören Haus und Straßen,
Mir ist ein weites Lager aufgebreitet,
Wovon den kleinsten Teil mir anzumaßen
Die Liebe rät, die alles wohl bereitet.
Ich zaudre noch, die Kerzen auszublasen,
Nun hör ich sie, wie leise sie auch gleitet,   70
Mit giergem Blick die Hochgestalt umschweif ich,
Sie legt sich bei, die Wohlgestalt ergreif ich.

VII

Not now! My aunt's downstairs, she listens when
I serve up here, and checks how long I stay;   50
She brandishes her cane, the old harridan,
And punishes each minute of delay.
But stay awake, don't lock your door, and then
When midnight comes, maybe we'll find a way.'
She wriggles free from my embrace, and slips
Back to her work; soon in again she trips

VIII

To serve me—but her looks, how much they tell!
A heavenly promise blossoms from her eyes;
I watch her rounded bosom's splendid swell
As it is filled with little half-checked sighs;   60
And to her ears and throat and neck as well
I see the fleeting rosy love-flush rise.
She pauses then, finds all her duties done,
Hesitates, looks about her and is gone.

IX

Now midnight's here; streets, houses are at rest;
My bed is wide, but I have settled for
The narrowest share of it, at the behest
Of Love, that all-foreseeing counsellor.
My candles burn still, as with daintiest
Of footfalls she comes gliding to my door.   70
Her lovely form I seize with eager eyes
And then with eager arms, as down she lies.

X

Sie macht sich los: Vergönne, daß ich rede,
Damit ich dir nicht völlig fremd gehöre.
Der Schein ist wider mich; sonst war ich blöde,
Stets gegen Männer setzt ich mich zur Wehre.
Mich nennt die Stadt, mich nennt die Gegend spröde;
Nun aber weiß ich, wie das Herz sich kehre:
Du bist mein Sieger, laß dichs nicht verdrießen,
Ich sah, ich liebte, schwur dich zu genießen.   80

XI

Du hast mich rein, und wenn ichs besser wüßte,
So gäb ichs dir, ich tue was ich sage.
So schließt sie mich an ihre süßen Brüste,
Als ob ihr nur an meiner Brust behage.
Und wie ich Mund und Aug und Stirne küßte,
So war ich doch in wunderbarer Lage:
Denn der so hitzig sonst den Meister spielet
Weicht schülerhaft zurück und abgekühlet.

XII

Ihr scheint ein süßes Wort, ein Kuß zu gnügen,
Als wär es alles was ihr Herz begehrte.   90
Wie keusch sie mir, mit liebevollem Fügen,
Des süßen Körpers Fülleform gewährte!
Entzückt und froh in allen ihren Zügen
Und ruhig dann, als wenn sie nichts entbehrte.
So ruht ich auch, gefällig sie beschauend,
Noch auf den Meister hoffend und vertrauend.

X

Still she withdraws: 'There's something I must tell
You, or we'll still be strangers! I know how
Things look to you, but please, try to think well
Of me. I've never gone with men till now;
They say I'm cold. I was a silly girl
Till I met you! But then I made a vow
That I would have you—yes, this very night!
You mustn't mind; I loved you at first sight;   80

XI

And I am still a virgin—otherwise
I'd not pretend; I've told you all I know.'
She hugs me close to her sweet breasts, and lies
There in my arms, happy at last. But though
I kissed her now, her mouth, her brow, her eyes,
I was in wondrous quandary even so:
My master player, hitherto so hot,
Shrinks, novice-like, its ardour quite forgot.

XII

How chaste she was! for though she made me free
Of her sweet body, loving words, a kiss   90
Contented her; she nestled close to me,
Desiring, as it seemed, no more than this;
Happy she looked, peacefully, yieldingly
Satisfied, as if nothing were amiss.
So I too lay and watched her, glad of heart,
Still hoping, trusting in that master part.

XIII

Doch als ich länger mein Geschick bedachte,
Von tausend Flüchen mir die Seele kochte,
Mich selbst verwünschend, grinsend mich belachte,
Nichts besser ward, wie ich auch zaudern mochte: 100
Da lag sie schlafend, schöner als sie wachte;
Die Lichter dämmerten mit langem Dochte.
Der Tages-Arbeit, jugendlicher Mühe
Gesellt sich gern der Schlaf und nie zu frühe.

XIV

So lag sie himmlisch an bequemer Stelle,
Als wenn das Lager ihr allein gehörte,
Und an die Wand gedrückt, gequetscht zur Hölle,
Ohnmächtig Jener, dem sie nichts verwehrte.
Vom Schlangenbisse fällt zunächst der Quelle
Ein Wandrer so, den schon der Durst verzehrte. 110
Sie atmet lieblich holdem Traum entgegen;
Er hält den Atem, sie nicht aufzuregen.

XV

Gefaßt bei dem, was ihm noch nie begegnet,
Spricht er zu sich: So mußt du doch erfahren,
Warum der Bräutigam sich kreuzt und segnet,
Vor Nestelknüpfen scheu sich zu bewahren.
Weit lieber da, wos Hellebarden regnet,
Als hier im Schimpf! So war es nicht vor Jahren,
Als deine Herrin dir zum ersten Male
Vors Auge trat im prachterhellten Saale. 120

XIII

But as I further pondered my mischance
I raged a thousandfold, my soul was rent
With cursing and self-mockery both at once:
Wait as I might, there was no betterment.   100
She slept, lovelier than waking innocence;
The candles flickered, their long wicks half-spent.
To youth, after a day's hard toil, the boon
Of willing slumber never comes too soon.

XIV

So the dear angel lies, and as if all
The bed were hers, spreads each commodious limb,
While he, still powerless, squashed against the wall,
Must forfeit what she freely offered him.
Thus a parched wanderer still is doomed to fall
By snakebite at the fountain's very rim.   110
She breathes in her sweet dreams, and for her sake
He holds his breath; she dreams and does not wake.

XV

Resigned to this most novel accident
He muses ruefully: So now you know
Why bridegrooms cross themselves, and what is meant
By magic love-knots.* Better a bloody foe
In battle than this shame! How different
Things once were with you, when long years ago
You met your lady,* on that first of nights,
In that glad throng, under the festive lights!   120

XVI

Da quoll dein Herz, da quollen deine Sinnen,
So daß der ganze Mensch entzückt sich regte.
Zum raschen Tanze trugst du sie von hinnen,
Die kaum der Arm und schon der Busen hegte,
Als wolltest du dir selbst sie abgewinnen;
Vervielfacht war, was sich für sie bewegte:
Verstand und Witz und alle Lebensgeister
Und rascher als die andern jener Meister.

XVII

So immerfort wuchs Neigung und Begierde,
Brautleute wurden wir im frühen Jahre,   130
Sie selbst des Maien schönste Blum und Zierde;
Wie wuchs die Kraft zur Lust im jungen Paare!
Und als ich endlich sie zur Kirche führte:
Gesteh ichs nur, vor Priester und Altare,
Vor deinem Jammerkreuz, blutrünstger Christe,
Verzeih mirs Gott! es regte sich der Iste.

XVIII

Und ihr, der Brautnacht reiche Bettgehänge,
Ihr Pfühle, die sich uns so breit erstreckten,
Ihr Teppiche, die Lieb und Lustgedränge
Mit seidenweichen Fittichen bedeckten,   140
Ihr Käfigvögel, deren Zwitschersänge
Zu neuer Lust und nie zu früh uns weckten,
Ihr kanntet uns, von eurem Schutz umfriedet,
Teilnehmend sie, mich immer unermüdet.

XVI

Oh then did not your soul and senses leap,
Was all of you not ecstasy at once?
Scarcely in your arms, already she was deep
Into your heart. Who clasped her in that dance
More jealously than you, as if to keep
Her even from yourself? Intelligence,
Wit, vital powers all doubled—but still faster
Was *its* increase, that little lord and master!

XVII

Thus still they grew, desire and tenderness;
We were betrothed in spring, and she was more   130
Lovely than any maytime's bloom; ah yes,
How strong it waxed, our youthful passion's store!
And when at last we wed, I do confess,
Before that altar and that priest, before
Thy wretched bloodstained cross, *domine Christe*,*
God pardon me! it stirred, young master Iste.*

XVIII

And you, the bridal bed's rich furnishings,
You pillows soft and wide for nuptial nights,
You woven fabrics with your silk-soft wings
Sheltering our bliss, our urgent lovers' rites;   140
You little cage-birds whose first twitterings,
Never too soon, woke us to fresh delights—
You knew us well, you saw how that kind soul
Received me as I played my tireless role.

XIX

Und wie wir oft sodann im Raub genossen
Nach Buhlenart des Ehstands heilge Rechte,
Von reifer Saat umwogt, vom Rohr umschlossen,
An manchem Unort, wo ichs mich erfrechte,
Wir waren augenblicklich, unverdrossen
Und wiederholt bedient vom braven Knechte!   150
Verfluchter Knecht, wie unerwecklich liegst du!
Und deinen Herrn ums schönste Glück betrügst du.

XX

Doch Meister Iste hat nun seine Grillen
Und läßt sich nicht befehlen noch verachten,
Auf einmal ist er da, und ganz im stillen
Erhebt er sich zu allen seinen Prachten.
So steht es nun dem Wandrer ganz zu Willen,
Nicht lechzend mehr am Quell zu übernachten.
Er neigt sich hin, er will die Schläfrin küssen,
Allein er stockt, er fühlt sich weggerissen.   160

XXI

Wer hat zur Kraft ihn wieder aufgestählet,
Als jenes Bild, das ihm auf ewig teuer,
Mit dem er sich in Jugendlust vermählet?
Dort leuchtet her ein frisch erquicklich Feuer,
Und wie er erst in Ohnmacht sich gequälet,
So wird nun hier dem Starken nicht geheuer.
Er schaudert weg, vorsichtig, leise, leise
Entzieht er sich dem holden Zauberkreise,

XIX

And then how often too, with wanton passion,
We'd furtively enjoy our married state!
Down in the waving corn, in shameless fashion,
Among the reeds our love we'd consummate,
And that good slave would give us double ration
Of service every time, early or late.   150
Now, thrice-accursèd slave, limp, lifeless toy,
You cheat your master of his dearest joy!

XX

But wise Sir Iste,* he has many a mood:
He'll not be bidden, he'll not be ignored.
For now, to his full, splendid magnitude,
He rears up quietly of his own accord;
Now sweet refreshment need not be eschewed,
Now the benighted wanderer's life's restored!
He turns to wake the maiden with a kiss—
But something checks him: what new scruple's this?   160

XXI

What (he reflects) has steeled his strength again
But *her* dear image, whom he took to wife
In lusty youth? He loves her, now as then;
From her it glows, this freshening fire of life.
So his new vigour troubles him—as when
He lay here helpless, he's once more in strife
Of mind. A certain dread now gives him pause;
From the charmed circle gently he withdraws,

XXII

Sitzt, schreibt: Ich nahte mich der heimschen Pforte,
Entfernen wollten mich die letzten Stunden,   170
Da hab ich nun, am sonderbarsten Orte,
Mein treues Herz aufs neue Dir verbunden.
Zum Schlusse findest du geheime Worte:
Die Krankheit erst bewähret den Gesunden.
Dies Büchlein soll dir manches Gute zeigen,
Das Beste nur muß ich zuletzt verschweigen.

XXIII

Da kräht der Hahn. Das Mädchen schnell entwindet
Der Decke sich und wirft sich rasch ins Mieder.
Und da sie sich so seltsam wiederfindet,
So stutzt sie, blickt und schlägt die Augen nieder —   180
Und da sie ihm zum letzten Mal verschwindet,
Im Auge bleiben ihm die schönen Glieder.
Das Posthorn tönt, er wirft sich in den Wagen
Und läßt getrost sich zu der Liebsten tragen.

XXIV

Und weil zuletzt bei jeder Dichtungsweise
Moralien uns ernstlich fördern sollen,
So will auch ich in so beliebtem Gleise
Euch gern bekennen, was die Verse wollen:
Wir stolpern wohl auf unsrer Lebensreise,
Und doch vermögen in der Welt, der tollen,   190
Zwei Hebel viel aufs irdische Getriebe:
Sehr viel die Pflicht, unendlich mehr die Liebe.

XXII

Sits, writes: 'Nearing my homeward journey's end,
In these last hours I have suffered some delay,   170
But my heart's true to you once more, dear friend,
And binds me to you in the strangest way.
Here some mysterious words I shall append:
Sickness is the true proof of health, they say.
This book shall tell you many a good thing,
But must not mention the best news I bring.'

XXIII

Now the day breaks. Quickly the girl leaps out
Of bed, throws on her clothes; waking in these
Strange circumstances, she's confused no doubt,
Looks up, and then looks down again. Now he's   180
Bidding goodbye to her; she turns about,
And as she leaves, her shapely limbs still please
His eye. The carriage waits, the posthorn's sound
Cheers him, he's soon homeward and wifeward bound.

XXIV

But since the end of all poetic art
Is the improvement of the reader's mind
(Or so we're told), my verses for their part
Shall point the usual moral of their kind:
This life's a crazy journey, and our heart
May stumble, but two mighty powers, we'll find,   190
Can move the world and help us as we go:
To Duty much, to Love far more we owe.*

XXII

Sirs, writes 'Nearing my homeward journey's end,
In these last hours I have suffered some delay;
But my Heart's sure region once more, dear friend,
And bids me to you in the straightest way.
Here some translations worth I shall append;
Sickness is the proof of health, they say.
This book shall tell you many a good thing,
But must not mention the great news I bring.

XXIII

Now the day breaks. Quickly she and leaps out
Of bed, throws on her clothes, waking in these
Strange circumstances, she's confused no doubt,
Looks up, and then looks down again. Now he's
Hiding good-bye to her, she turns about,
And as she leaves, her shapely limbs still please
His eye. The carriage waits, the platform's sound
Cheers him, he's soon homeward and wishward bound.

XXIV

But since the end of all poetic art
Is the improvement of the readers mind
(Once we're told) my verses for their part
Shall point the moral moral of their kind;
This life's a crazy journey, and our heart
May stumble; but two mighty powers, we'll find,
Can move the world and help us as we go.
To Duty much, to Love far more we owe.

TRANSLATOR'S POSTSCRIPT

The *Roman Elegies* and *Venetian Epigrams* are here translated into English accentual elegiacs, a metre intended to approximate to Goethe's German accentual elegiacs, which in their turn are no more than an approximation to the quantitative elegiacs of classical Greek and Latin. In ancient 'quantitative' verse the syllables are either 'long' (–) or 'short' ($^\cup$), whereas in Goethe's as in all other modern imitations this distinction is simply equated with that between stressed (/) and unstressed ($^\times$) syllables, although in fact it is a matter of controversy how quantity was related to stress in the ancient languages. But subject to this fundamental difference and given this interpretation of the model, Goethe follows it with reasonable strictness. The conventions which he evidently felt to be essential if a minimal sense of the specific 'elegiac' metre was to be retained may be listed as follows:

1. The verse is invariably in distichs (two-line units) each consisting of a hexameter followed by a pentameter.

2. The hexameter contains neither more nor less than six 'feet', each of which (with certain exceptions as specified below) may be either a dactyl (–$^{\cup\cup}$, /$^{\times\times}$) or a spondee (– –, //).

3. The sixth foot of the hexameter always has only two syllables and is thus never a dactyl. In Greek or Latin its second syllable was either long (making it a spondee) or short (making it in effect a trochee, –$^\cup$, though some theorists describe this as a catalectic dactyl). In modern accentual imitations the so-called spondee in any case constantly tends to degenerate into a trochee, the latter rhythm (/$^\times$) being therefore much the commoner one in disyllabic feet, whether at the end of the hexameter or elsewhere.

4. The penultimate foot of the hexameter must be a dactyl, i.e. the hexameter ends /$^{\times\times}$/(/), not ///(/).

5. The pentameter has a fixed central 'caesura' or (at least notional) break, which divides it symmetrically into two half-lines (hemistichs) each of two and a half feet, the last syllable of each hemistich therefore being always 'long' (stressed).

6. In no case does any line, or the second hemistich of any pentameter, begin with an unstressed syllable (anacrusis).

7. The second hemistich of the pentameter must contain two dactyls, i.e. it is always $/^{\times\times}/^{\times\times}/$.

There was also the question of whether the German hexameter, like the pentameter, must or could contain a caesura, and if so where; by ancient theory it was supposed to, with permitted variations of position. Goethe seems largely to have left this point to take care of itself, though in practice his at least notional hexameter-caesura usually falls as a natural enough break after the first or (if it is a dactyl) second syllable of the third foot.

In general, while recognizing these conventions, Goethe observes them with a certain nonchalance, and seems not always quite certain what they require. He would often seek, or at least receive, prosodic advice from learned friends, but even after accepting it he would tend to rely after all on his own instinct and revert to his original version. The results are not always metrically satisfactory, especially in the *Venetian Epigrams*, which are a less finished product than the *Elegies*. A syllable obviously short and unstressed in German is fairly often forced to do duty as long or stressed, and vice versa. Thus for example 'Alles, was ihr wollt, ich . . .' (36) is really not acceptable as the three spondees it is supposed to be, nor does 'Rein und unrein zeigt . . .' (20) work well as the first half of a pentameter; equally, in the *Elegies*, the second syllable of 'Theseus' (XV) and the fourth syllable of 'Violettstrumpf' (VIII) are hard to pronounce as shorts. On the whole, however, the tension between the formal metre and the natural speech-rhythms was salutary: Goethe's distichs benefited from the compromises to which his ear guided him. Given his purpose of writing erotic poetry in stylized classical verse, he felt he had discovered in the elegiac conventions a law which paradoxically served his liberating project and made a new stylistic synthesis possible. As Emil Staiger pointed out in his masterly study,[1] a verse-form regulated in certain ways, but requiring no rhyme, was one in which he could obey rules while virtually improvising. It may be significant, as Staiger suggests, that Goethe always avoided the appreciably more difficult four-line strophic forms of ancient

[1] *Goethe* (Atlantis Verlag, Zurich, 1956), ii. 66 f.

poetry, much as he admired Horace and Catullus and their other great practitioners. Could the balance between liberty and convention have been preserved, could the syllables of alcaics or asclepiads have been counted out with his fingers on his sleeping mistress's back, as he tells us his hexameters were (VII, 149 f.)? He never seems to have tried it; but hexameters and pentameters he used with fluency and relish for many years. He delighted, for instance, in the neat devices of antithesis and chiasmus to which the distich and especially the symmetrical pentameter lend themselves (as in VII, 140 and 144; 'Werd ich auch halb nur gelehrt, bin ich doch doppelt beglückt . . .', 'Sehe mit fühlendem Aug, fühle mit sehender Hand . . .'). As Goethe well knew, such felicities are directly inspired by the metrical rule which he had embraced.

If this urbane, ironic, and unpompous flavour of informality within a formal convention is to be appreciated, anyone reading the *Elegies* aurally or aloud must adopt a reasonably tactful and flexible interpretation of the relative stresses and speeds within the lines. The same is meant to apply to the present English version, which seeks to retain something of the original's characteristic qualities by fairly closely observing most of the 'minimum' rules of elegiacs listed above, while not attempting to be less liberal about them than Goethe was. For example I have tried throughout to retain the essential fixed caesura of the pentameter or at least to suggest its pattern of two hemistichs even when there is in practice no appreciable break between them. In VII, 144 the pentameter 'Seeing with vision that feels, feeling with fingers that see' clearly shows its symmetrical structure, which the natural speech-rhythm supports; in VII, 146 on the other hand ('Hours of night as a rich recompense she can bestow') the required stress and caesura are notional rather than actual, though 'rich recompense' should be read in such a way as not to destroy them altogether. In English, appropriate scansions can often be unobtrusively suggested by an accommodating enunciation of the words, mainly because so many English vowels are diphthongal or triphthongal: thus 'hours' in the line just quoted may be read disyllabically (making 'hours of' a suggested dactyl). Similar treatment is invited by pentameter-endings which would otherwise be too spondaic (rule 7), such as 'with corn-ears wreathed' in XIV, 266 and 'encircling arm' in XV, 320; and on the same principle, a word such as 'tedious' or 'odious' occurring as the last foot of a hexameter would be read as having not three syllables but two (rule 3).

The required scansion of lines is generally obvious in Latin or Greek or even German, but less so in English, in which the pre-dominance of monosyllabic words makes for metrical ambiguity. Unless the obtrusive device of written stress accents is adopted it becomes difficult, merely by the speech-rhythms of English, to guide the reader in the right prosodic direction. The language's lack of inflection and therefore comparatively rigid word-order is a fur-ther problem. Nevertheless it is not true, though often asserted, that English accentual hexameters and pentameters must inevitably sound unnatural or faintly ridiculous, and that in order to produce a tolerable English equivalent of such lines their prosodic basis must be virtually abandoned. I have sought to avoid lending colour to this comfortable theory, which was in any case disproved by W. H. Auden in his poem 'Natural Linguistics' (1969), an effortless metri-cal analogue of correct elegiacs and a model example of the kind of equivalent I am here attempting.

In the *Roman Elegies*, a still relatively young poet in his first 'classical' years was for the first time deliberately attaching himself to a stylistic tradition centuries old, and finding that its yoke was easy and its burden light. In *Das Tagebuch*, written about twenty years later, the long-since mature master was setting himself, and accomplishing with sovereign ease, an even more sophisticated met-rical task. The significance of Goethe's choice for this poem of the *ottava rima* stanza, a metre he infrequently used, has already been discussed in the Introduction. Another example of it is the opening 'Dedication' in *Faust*. The prosodic conventions of *ottava rima* are clearer than those of elegiac verse and probably less unfamiliar to most modern readers. An Italian invention like so many forms of rhymed verse, it was brought to perfection and great prominence as the established metre of the high Renaissance epic (Ariosto and Tasso in Italy, Camões in Portugal). Its unvarying scheme of eight iambic five-foot lines rhyming ab ab ab cc presents no great diffi-culty in the Romance languages, but in German and especially in English, with fewer rhyming words to choose from, the problem is harder to solve. Moreover, a strict imitation of the Italian norm of hendecasyllabic lines would require the rhymes to be 'feminine' throughout. This is essentially alien to English verse, and in practice masculine rhyming has been allowed to predominate in English imitations of *ottava rima*, as well as in its slightly more elaborate variant the Spenserian stanza. It is significant that the major English example of the form, Byron's satirical epic *Don Juan*, uses feminine rhymes as lavishly and as ingeniously as possible, but that the effect is usually one of deliberately facetious self-parody. In German the difficulty is less acute, and thanks largely to Goethe a compromise was achieved: in every case of his use of the *ottava* metre, except one, he adopted a strict alternation of feminine and masculine rhymes (i.e. of hendecasyllabic and decasyllabic lines), and this established itself as the standard German practice.

The single exception was *Das Tagebuch*, one of the remarkable features of which is that throughout its twenty-four stanzas the rhymes are feminine, the Italian hendecasyllabic model is followed exactly. It is rather as if Goethe had reserved for this poem, which he knew he could never publish, the same virtuosity as he was to show in his only two excursions into the even more exacting metre of *terza rima*, the linking ternary form (aba bcb cdc ded, etc.) made famous by Dante. Late in 1826, in his seventy-eighth year, a new German translation of the *Divine Comedy* inspired him to write the solemn meditation 'On Contemplating Schiller's Skull' and Faust's splendid speech greeting the sunrise at the beginning of *Faust Part Two*, both of which not only follow Dante's rhyme-scheme but are also hendecasyllabic throughout. The *ottava rima* of *Das Tagebuch* is ultra-strict in the same way, and in translating it I should greatly have liked to be able to imitate this, as a distinctive element in the poem's specific character. But just as there are fewer feminine rhymes in German than in Italian, so also there are far fewer in English than in German; German has therefore always been able to make much greater use of hendecasyllables and in general to follow more demanding conventions. (Stefan George's fastidiously hendecasyllabic translation of selections from Dante in 1909 is another outstanding example.) In English, when the *ottava* or *terza* rhyme-scheme has been adopted at all (as in the classic translations of Ariosto and Tasso or some versions of Dante), the hendecasyllabic observance seems always to have been regarded as impossible, or in any case at variance with the spirit of the language.

I regretfully decided that it would also be impossible here, even in a shorter poem and notwithstanding such translator's licences as overrunning and paraphrase; accordingly I have conformed to the English tradition and imitated Goethe's feminine endings only in a minority of cases.

EXPLANATORY NOTES

ROMAN ELEGIES

I The significance of the two hitherto usually suppressed 'Priapic' Elegies I and XXIV is explained and discussed in the Introduction. Both are modelled on the Latin *Carmina Priapea*, the first-century collection of highly indecent epigrams in honour of the phallic god Priapus (see Introduction p. xxiv and note), and it is very probable that Goethe originally intended them to stand as prologue and epilogue to the *Erotica Romana*, as the *Roman Elegies* were originally called. It is true that there is no known MS in which the two Priapic poems actually appear as numbers I and XXIV, framing a sequence of twenty-four, and no evidence that he ever submitted them for publication to the prudish or at least cautious Schiller, who found even numbers III and XVII too *risqué* for his new journal. The MS submitted for *Die Horen* in October 1794 (an autograph in Latin script, listed by the WA as H50) contained twenty-two elegies, which were then reduced to twenty when Goethe reluctantly withdrew III and XVII rather than bowdlerize them as Schiller had suggested. He then did not bother to renumber the remaining twenty poems consequentially, but left the MS in a state of confusion. Nevertheless, to preserve the rejected items, he made a fair copy of III and XVII, added to this a fair copy of the two Priapic elegies, also in Latin script, and kept all four (which were never to be published in his lifetime) in a separate MS notebook (H51), numbering them 'Elegie I', 'Elegie II', 'Elegie III', and 'Elegie IV'. This pointed collocation of III, XVII, I, and XXIV is the best MS evidence we have that there is a close association between the two *priapica* and the *Erotica Romana* or *Roman Elegies*. This evidence is further corroborated by the clear allusion in the first distich of the first Priapic elegy to a cycle (a 'garden') of poems (see below). Accordingly, despite the undoubted difference of tone between these two phallic jests and the more seriously personal 'flowers of love' which they enclose, we have felt authorized both to place them as the first and last poems of the cycle and to designate them as Prologue and Epilogue.

Priapus (his name is stressed on the second syllable in Latin, German, and English) was a fertility-god whose cult spread from Asia Minor to Greece in Hellenistic times; according to the Greeks his parents were the wine-god Dionysus (Bacchus) and the love-goddess Aphrodite (Venus) (see Elegy XIII). The Romans adopted him as a god of gardens, in which his comically ithyphallic statue would be set up as a kind of combined scarecrow (see Elegy XIX) and tutelary deity. (He survives today as the sentimentalized and of course de-phallicized 'garden gnome'.) In Elegies I and XXIV Goethe takes over and develops some of the stock motifs of the *Priapea*, notably the conventional symbolic parallel between a book and a garden, poems and the fruit which Priapus is appointed to guard (as in *Carmina Priapea* II, LX, etc.), and the phallic penalties (ibid., XXII, XXIV, LXXII) which the guardian will inflict on unwanted intruders. Thus in the opening poem Goethe introduces his cycle of erotic verse as a 'garden of love', neatly divided into separate flowerbeds (elegies) and watched over by the god; the 'marauders' are hypocritical readers who will be offended (compare *Priapea* XLIX) by these poems which are 'fruits of pure Nature'; they are accordingly threatened with an 'unnatural' sexual assault.

For the *Elegies* as they appeared (without I, III, XVII, and XXIV) in the 1815 edition of his collected works, Goethe added a two-line rhymed epigraph:

> Wie wir einst so glücklich waren!
> Müssens erst durch euch erfahren.
>
> We were happy once; and now
> Let my verse remind us how.

I, 1 *flowers of Eros*: on the translation of *Liebe* see note on III, 29.

II, 12 *Genius, how idly you sleep*: this hemistich has usually been understood as an invocation of the *genius loci* (translatable therefore as: 'Spirit of Rome, are you dumb?'). As suggested in the Introduction, however, it is possible in the present context that Goethe is covertly and ironically invoking Eros-Priapus, as the 'spirit' of Rome both ancient and modern.

III, 29 *Eros*: constant reference to the personification of sexual love ('amor') was part of the Latin stylistic convention which Goethe is imitating. He consistently calls the love-god either simply 'Liebe' or uses, as here, his Latin name 'Amor' (scanned in German as a trochee); in the *Elegies* generally, however, he does not exclude the Greek names for the gods ('Zeus' appearing occasionally for Jupiter and 'Hermes' regularly replacing Mercury). 'Cupid' would be a correct English translation of 'Amor', but I have preferred 'Eros' (with the anglicized pronunciation) as being also trochaic but slightly more flexible.

III, 37 f. *Princess Borghese . . . Nipotina*: well-known Roman beauties of more recent times, married respectively to Prince Marcantonio Borghese and to the papal nepote Count Braschi.

IV, 57 ff. *Now at last . . . pursuit*: the first four distichs of this elegy origi-
nally read:

> Fraget nun, wen ihr auch wollt, mich werdet ihr nimmer erreichen,
>   Schöne Damen, und ihr, Herren der feineren Welt!
> Ob denn auch Werther gelebt? Ob denn auch alles fein wahr sei?
>   Welche Stadt sich mit Recht Lottens, der einzigen, rühmt?
> Ach, wie hab ich so oft die törichten Blätter verwünscht,
>   Die mein jugendlich Leid unter die Menge gebracht!
> Wäre Werther mein Bruder gewesen, ich hätt ihn erschlagen,
>   Kaum verfolgte mich so rächend sein trauriger Geist . . .

> Now at last I am safe from you all! Go elsewhere with your
>   questions,
>   My fair ladies, my fine gentlemen of the *beau monde*!
> Was there really a Werther? and is the book the true story?
>   In which town did the dear Lotte in fact really live?
> Foolish pages! alas, how often I've cursed you: you spread my
>   Youthful sorrow abroad, made it the talk of the world!
> Even if Werther had been my brother and if I had killed him—
>   I'd have been scarcely so plagued by his avenging sad ghost! . . .

Goethe later altered these revealingly personal lines, which allude to
the simplistic popular view of him as above all else the author of *The
Sorrows of Young Werther* (1774). By the time of the *Elegies* he had
outgrown the romantic sensibility of his youthful novel, the fame of
which caused him lifelong embarrassment.

IV, 65 ff. *Malbrouk*: a satirical song about the Duke of Marlborough, begin-
ning 'Malbrouk s'en va-t-en guerre . . .', was in the 1780s tediously
popular all over Europe.

IV, 70, 74 *the mob . . . folly of kings . . . Gallic frenzy*: alluding to the French
Revolution.

V, 93 *Anchises*: the Trojan prince whom Venus took as her lover, and who
thus became the father of the hero Aeneas.

V, 95 *Endymion*: a shepherd boy, loved by Diana.

V, 97 *Leander*: the young man from Abydos who fell in love with Hero, the
priestess of Aphrodite at Sestos, and swam every night to her across the
Hellespont, finally perishing in a storm.

V, 99 *Rhea Sylvia*: a Vestal virgin seduced by Mars; their children Romulus
and Remus were exposed to starve but were suckled by a she-wolf and
lived to become the legendary founders of Rome.

VI, 117 *whirled on a wheel or chained to a cliff-face*: alluding to the fates of Ixion (who had tried to seduce Juno) and of Prometheus (who had stolen the secret of fire from the gods to give it to men).

VI, 121 *Proteus . . . Thetis*: a sea-god and sea-goddess noted for their ability to transform themselves into various shapes.

VI, 127 *Thus . . . she appeared to me*: Goethe may be alluding to his first meeting with Christiane-'Faustina' and to her attractive hairstyle, which figures prominently in his drawings of her (see for example the reproductions of these in Beutler, 'Christiane', opposite p. 256 and Boyle, *Goethe*, opposite p. 397). The passage also echoes late Roman allegorical descriptions of the 'goddess Opportunity' as wearing her hair short behind and long in front, to encourage men to seize her (as we still say) 'by the forelock'.

VII, 137 f. *counsels . . . of the ancients*: probably alluding to the advice of Horace to his readers (*De arte poetica*, 268 f.):

> vos exemplaria Graeca
> nocturna versate manu, versate diurna.

> Let the works of the Greeks be
> Held in your hands each day, each night let your hands still explore
> them.

VII, 154 *Triumvirs, the three poets of Love*: Goethe's acknowledged models for the *Elegies* were the Latin erotic poets Gaius Valerius Catullus (*c*.84–54 BC), Albius Tibullus (*c*.48–19 BC), and Sextus Propertius (*c*.48–15 BC). The Renaissance philologist Scaliger called them the 'triumviri amoris'.

VIII, 160 *the husband I lost*: 'Faustina' is a widow with a young child. It is interesting in this connection that on his return from Italy in 1788 Goethe is reported as telling his Weimar friends that 'in Rome there is no debauchery with unmarried women, but it is all the more customary with the married ones' (letter from Schiller to Körner, 7 September 1788). A young widow would presumably have been an even better choice, and this lends plausibility to the status here apparently ascribed to the poet's fictionalized mistress, given the inaccessibility of virgins and the risk of venereal disease with prostitutes (cf. XVII and XXI).

VIII, 168 f. *Falconieri . . . Albani*: names of well-known Roman families; it is uncertain, and immaterial, whether any allusion to specific persons is intended.

VIII, 172 *scarlet and purple*: the colours of gaiters worn by cardinals and bishops.

VIII, 182 *Her little boy*: see note to l. 160.

IX, 192 *wearisome world*: the MS contains at this point the following additional distich, which Goethe deleted before publication:

Da ein trauriges Bette dem darbenden Armen vergebens
    Lohn der einsamen Nacht, ruhige Stunden, verhieß

Poor frustrated wretch! through those lonely nights on my cheerless
    Bed I would vainly await sleep as their only reward.

IX, 202 *guest-honouring Jove*: among the numerous epithets of Zeus was 'xenios', indicating that the relationship between host and guest was sacred to him; the Romans correspondingly called him 'Jupiter hospes' or 'hospitalis'.

IX, 203 *goddess of Youth*: Hebe, who welcomed Hercules to Olympus.

IX, 209 *god of Hospitality*: see note to l. 202.

IX, 213 *Hermes*: the reference to Hermes (Mercury) here concerns his function as the god who guided the souls of the dead to the underworld (but cf. XVII).

IX, 214 *Cestius' tomb*: the so-called Pyramid of Cestius beside the Protestant cemetery. Goethe is on record as having imagined during his stay in Rome that he might die there and be buried in its shadow; his son August was in fact buried in this cemetery in 1830.

XII, 231 *Henry and Frederick*: Henri IV of France (1553-1610), and (probably) Friedrich II of Prussia ('Frederick the Great', 1712-86) who had recently died.

XIII this elegy, placed at a central point in the cycle, is closely related to I and XXIV in that all three are in honour of Priapus (cf. Introduction), though XIII expresses this homage in a disguised and contrived manner whereas the other two do so more openly. In XIII the poet implicitly compares himself to a sculptor, as in XXIV. A sculptor's workshop is like a pantheon of deities, and among them are Bacchus (Dionysus) and Venus (Aphrodite, Cythere), the parents of the phallic god whose statue they miss; the artist will respond by supplying one. Similarly, the poet writes erotic elegies which celebrate sensuous joy, and which can take their rightful place among other and more solemn poetic forms. Having thus artistically rehabilitated the erotic principle, he lays his poems on the altar of the Graces in gratitude for their favour.

XIV, 249 *Via Flaminia*: Goethe's lodging in Rome was near the Porta del Popolo, from which the Via Flaminia runs northwards into the Campagna.

XIV, 252 *Ceres*: the Roman name for Demeter, the goddess of agriculture; before being enlightened by her, men subsisted not on corn or other 'cereals', but on more primitive nourishment such as acorns.

XIV, 258 *Eleusis*: the place near Athens at which the 'Eleusinian Mysteries' were celebrated for many centuries. Demeter had supposedly lived for some time at Eleusis and on her departure founded these orgiastic rites, which also honoured the god Dionysus (Bacchus) and Demeter's daughter Persephone (Proserpina). The Romans did not fully adopt this cult until the time of the Emperor Hadrian, when Greece had long been a province under the Roman conquest.

XIV, 273 *Jasion*: scanned here as a dactyl, though strictly it should be stressed on the last syllable. The association of this particular amour of Demeter's (of which an account is given by Ovid) with the Eleusinian festival is an invention by Goethe.

XV the fact that Goethe published this elegy in 1791 (see below), in isolation and before the rest of the cycle, may mean that he considered it specially important.

XV, 315 *friend of the Muses*: proverbially, 'Aurora' is 'Musis amica'.

XV, 321 f. *Has your memorial been raised*: the text, and with it the meaning, of this distich has throughout almost the whole publication history of the *Roman Elegies* been editorially misrepresented, and we are here restoring from Goethe's manuscript exactly what (to judge from the available facsimiles) he originally wrote in 1790. As it happens, the authenticity of this version is also corroborated by the first isolated printing of the poem. In July 1791 Goethe published Elegy XV, by itself and before any of the others, in *Deutsche Monatsschrift*, a literary periodical edited by his friend Karl Philipp Moritz, and in this first published text the distich 321 f. was punctuated exactly as in the autograph (H50): with an exclamation mark after *Erwachen* and a question mark after *gewiegt*. This correct punctuation then disappeared from the editorial canon, not even rating a mention as a variant reading in the textual apparatus of the WA. It has reappeared more recently in certain specialized separate editions of the *Elegies* which are based on the manuscripts (A. Leitzmann (1912), M. Hecker (1920), D. Jost (1974), H.-G. Dewitz (1980); see Bibliography), though its significance was perceived only by Hecker. The punctuation as such might seem a negligible point, if it did not radically affect the meaning of the lines. The original rhetorical question in the past indicative tense ('Erhieltet ihr . . .?'), as the poet wakes in delight beside the still sleeping Faustina, quite clearly alludes to the still erect, or again erect, 'memorial' or 'monument' of their recent pleasures. As Hecker puts it in the notes to his facsimile edition (p. 46): 'These lines can only mean that "Master Iste" (as *The Diary* calls him . . .) has maintained himself in and beyond sleep in "his full splendour".' It is interesting that Hecker quotes in this context the phallic-narcissistic phrase 'in allen seinen Prachten' from *The Diary* (l. 156), rather as if he had intuitively grasped the central thematic link between *The Diary* and the *Roman Elegies* (see above, Introduction p. xxxiv, etc.), a link which it has taken nearly two centuries to retrieve.

In Schiller's *Horenfassung* (1795) and all the canonical editions that followed it, the punctuation of this crucial distich has been edited: the supposedly definitive WA version replaces the exclamation mark in 321 with a comma, which permits and indeed requires *erhieltet* to be read as a past subjunctive (optative); furthermore, the closing question mark in 322 has disappeared, becoming either a meaningless full stop (*Horenfassung*, Eibl) or the generally accepted exclamation mark of the WA. It is true that eighteenth-century punctuation conventions did not strictly require question marks at the end of rhetorical questions, but the sense of these words as a rhetorical question is nevertheless quite plain. The main traditional error, given credence by the WA, has been to read the distich as

> Welch ein freudig Erwachen, erhieltet ihr, ruhige Stunden,
>   Mir das Denkmal der Lust, die in den Schlaf uns gewiegt!

This version will not survive careful scrutiny of the MS, but for the guardians of the Family Goethe, determined at least to exclude his penis from the scenario, it had the advantage of enabling the passage to be understood in a relatively decent sense. The optative exclamation 'how joyfully I should wake if [the] quiet night hours *were to* preserve' (or perhaps 'were to have preserved') 'a memorial of the pleasure that rocked us to sleep!' could henceforth be taken to refer to a *literary* 'memorial', indeed this was now arguably its only possible meaning: the hope that life might be transformed into art, that a poem celebrating the night's doings—gestated perhaps in the 'quiet night hours'—might be helped to completion by the dawn which is *Musis amica*, and remain as the *Denkmal der Lust*. The close thematic association in the *Elegies* between love-making and artistic creativity (as in VII, above all) made this a quite plausible interpretation; unfortunately, it interpreted the wrong text. Jost (p. 173) varies it to identify the 'memorial' with the *Elegies* as a whole; in Eibl's desperate conjecture (i. 1116) the *Denkmal* is the body of the sleeping girl. With the honourable exception of Max Hecker, modern editors have ignored the phallic meaning. In the present edition we restore the text of Goethe's MS and of the first printing (1791), together with the sense it clearly demands. It is interesting in this connection to recall Thomas Mann's imaginative reconstruction of Goethe's later life in the novel *Lotte in Weimar*, chapter 7 of which introduces the elderly poet with a remarkable interior monologue as he wakes in the early morning: his first thoughts are of an erotic dream to the bodily 'monument' of which he addresses congratulatory remarks.

XV, 332 *Ariadne*: one of the daughters of King Minos of Crete, who helped the hero Theseus to kill the Minotaur in its labyrinth; he then abducted her, but abandoned her as she lay asleep on the island of Naxos, where Bacchus later found and consoled her.

XVII, 343 *Python*: the dragon killed by Apollo at Delphi.

XVII, 343 *Hydra*: another monster, with nine heads and living in a swamp at Lerna; it was killed by the hero Hercules (cf. XXII) as one of his Twelve Labours.

XVII, 348 *new monster*: Goethe makes the traditional assumption that syphilis was unknown in Europe before medieval times; in the absence of evidence to the contrary this view is still generally accepted. There is also no evidence that Goethe himself ever contracted any venereal disease, though the number of his contemporaries who did included his patron Duke Karl August of Weimar, as we learn from Goethe's letter to him of 6 April 1789, in which he refers to this Elegy.

XVII, 351 *Hesperian dragon*: the serpent Ladon which kept watch over the tree of golden apples in the garden of the 'daughters of the west' (Hesperides).

XVII, 357 *Lucretius*: Titus Lucretius Carus (d. 55 BC), author of the didactic epic *De rerum natura*, in which he recommends sexual promiscuity (IV, 1063 ff.).

XVII, 359 *Propertius*: cf. note on VII, 154; 'Cynthia' was the fictional name of his mistress.

XVII, 370 *Semele*: the mother of Bacchus by Jupiter, who destroyed her by appearing to her in his true form as the god of thunder and lightning.

XVII, 370 *Callisto*: another of Jupiter's mistresses, whom he concealed by turning her into a she-bear, and later raised to the heavens as a constellation.

XVII, 373 *Juno*: the wife of Jupiter, always jealous of his infidelities (see also XXII).

XVII, 378 *Mercury . . . knows the cure*: derivatives of mercury (quicksilver) were in the eighteenth century widely believed to be effective for the treatment of syphilis.

XVIII, 389 f. *Caesar . . . Florus*: according to Hadrian's biographer Spartian, the poet Florus had composed an epigram to the effect that he would not wish to be the emperor, engaged in arduous travel and military expeditions which even exposed him to the British climate; Hadrian had replied in a counter-epigram that he would not change his lot for that of Florus who spends his time in low Roman taverns and eating-houses being bitten by fleas.

XVIII, 394 *Osterie*: wine-taverns, the word being 'fittingly' derived from *oste* (landlord); cf. the English 'hostelry'.

XVIII, 395 *her uncle*: the Latin poets commonly assign to an uncle (*patruus*) the role of watching over and censuring the morals of his nephews and nieces (see also XIX).

XVIII, 403 *Over the table it spilled*: the theme of assignations or other amorous messages written surreptitiously in wine on the table-top was common in the Latin poets. Ovid for instance writes in the *Heroides* (17. 87):

> orbe quoque in mensae legi sub nomine nostro
> quod deducta mero littera fecit AMO.

> And what is more, on the round table-top where you'd written my name out
> In the wine, you would add letters composing I LOVE.

and in the *Ars amatoria* (1. 571–2):

> Blanditiasque leves tenui perscribere vino
> Ut dominam in mensa se legat illa tuam.

> And in a film of wine you may write some affectionate message,
> So on the table she'll read she is the lady you love.

Cf. also *Amores* 1. 4. 20 and 2. 5. 17, likewise Tibullus 1. 6. 18 f. and Propertius 3. 8. 25.

XVIII, 410 *'IV'*: the assignation is made for 'four' o'clock according to the old system of time-keeping which (as Goethe notes in his *Italian Journey*) was still in use in eighteenth-century Rome, i.e. for the fourth hour after nightfall.

XVIII, 416 *Horace . . . foretold*: Horace (*Carmen saeculare* 11–12) declares that the sun will never have seen anything greater than the city of Rome.

XVIII, 428 *Fortunate robbers*: probably alluding to the legend of how Romulus' men, at the time of the foundation of Rome, forcibly carried off the women of the neighbouring Sabine tribe.

XIX this elegy again introduces the theme of the watchful uncle (cf. XVII), as well as that of the scarecrow and the sexual symbolism of the garden (cf. I, XXIV).

XXI, 464 *serpents and poison*: Goethe reverts here to the theme of venereal disease developed in XVII.

XXII, 480 *Repute*: 'Fama' (the word literally means spoken report, rumour, hence also repute, reputation, fame) was personified as a malignant and unpleasant goddess by Latin poets, notably by Vergil (*Aeneid* 4. 173 ff., where she spreads abroad the amour of Dido and Aeneas); Ovid also describes her as living in a 'brazen' tower (*Metamorphoses* 12. 39 ff.). Goethe's story of her feud with Cupid is an inventive recombination of various classical motifs.

XXII, 488 *Hercules*: the demigod Hercules was born to Alcmene, wife of the Theban general Amphitryon, after Jupiter had seduced her by impersonating her husband.

XXII, 488 *Hercules now is my slave*: i.e. he is now concerned only with fame and self-glorification.

XXII, 491 *Alcmene*: see note to l. 488.

XXII, 499 *the Amazon's victor*: one of the Twelve Labours of Hercules was to rob the Amazon queen Hippolyta of her girdle.

XXII, 504 *a fair lady*: requiring healing and purification after his great deeds, Hercules was told by the Delphic oracle that he must sell himself into servitude for three years; accordingly he became a slave of Omphale, queen of Lydia. During this time Omphale is said to have amused herself by wearing the hero's lion-skin costume, and he by dressing up as a woman and using a spinning-wheel. Descendants of Hercules later became kings of Lydia.

XXII, 521 *Vulcan*: in the story told by Homer the god Vulcan, a skilled metalsmith, invented a booby-trapped bed to catch his wife Venus with her lover Mars, to the vast amusement of the other gods. Goethe had always relished this famous episode (*Odyssey* 7. 267 ff.), and had alluded to it in an interesting symbolic way in one of his early Storm and Stress poems (see the analysis of 'Künstlers Morgenlied' by Hans Rudolf Vaget, 'Eros und Apoll', in *Jahrbuch der Schillergesellschaft*, 30 (1986)).

XXII, 547 f. *the old rule . . . the Greeks paid for it*: quoting Horace's comment (*Epistolae* 1. 2, 14) on the Trojan war as recounted in Homer's *Iliad* ('quidquid delirant reges, plectuntur Achivi').

XXIII, 556 *Midas*: Ovid (*Metamorphoses* 11. 174 ff.) tells the story of how King Midas of Phrygia, for criticizing Apollo's musicianship, had his ears changed into those of an ass. He was able to conceal them from everyone except his barber, but the latter, as a compromise with the oath of silence that burdened him, eventually dug a hole in the earth and whispered the secret into it, whereupon reeds grew up at this spot and murmured into the wind, the matter thus becoming public knowledge.

XXIV the cycle closes with the second of the two openly 'Priapic' elegies (cf. I and Introduction). In this epilogue Priapus himself speaks, to thank the poet for rehabilitating him (as his parents Bacchus and Venus had wished in XIII). Now that the *Roman Elegies* have been written, he is no longer a dilapidated old wooden image in a forgotten and neglected garden: 'the artist' has made him a smart new statue of more durable material (l. 14), and honoured by all and sundry. In gratitude, the god now blesses the poet's sexual prowess (which on another level, as in *The Diary*, also represents his creative power).

XXIV, 602 *Philaenis*: a courtesan to whom the authorship of a well-known ancient erotic manual was attributed. The phrase, coming significantly in this final distich of the *Roman Elegies*, is a direct quotation from the *Priapea* (no. LXIII): 'tot figurae, quot Philaenis enarrat', i.e. as many sexual positions as she describes.

VENETIAN EPIGRAMS

In the 1815 edn. of Goethe's works the *Venetian Epigrams* (still officially *Epigramme: Venedig 1790*) were like the *Roman Elegies* introduced by a rhymed epigraph:

> Wie man Geld und Zeit vertan,
> Zeigt das Büchlein lustig an.

> Wasted time, an open purse,
> Made this jolly book of verse.

1 *Pagan burial-urns . . . satyr*: like the Priapic introduction to the *Roman Elegies*, this celebration of the 'pagan' sensuous fullness of life and art stands fittingly at the beginning of a cycle of largely erotic poetry by which the poet hopes to live on even in death. Bacchants or bacchantes were the female followers of Dionysus (Bacchus), the god of wine and ecstasy, by whom they were stirred into mystic frenzy; the god was also attended by the semi-animal creatures known as fauns to the Romans and satyrs to the Greeks. As a long epigram or short elegy, this poem illustrates the fluidity of the distinction between the two forms since ancient times. Another example (here omitted) of the extended elegiac epigram is Goethe's grateful poetic tribute to his patron and friend

Karl August, 'Klein ist unter den Fürsten Germaniens freilich der meine . . .' ('No great prince, to be sure, is my prince among Germany's rulers . . .'); he inserted it into his 1800 edition of the Venetian cycle, in which it has since then often been included, though strictly speaking it was written earlier and was originally intended as one of the *Roman Elegies*.

2 *still draws me northwards*: this and several other epigrams (such as 30, 35, 36, 37) express Goethe's regret at having had to leave Weimar, Christiane and their baby son, his tender recollections of her pregnancy, etc.

4 *contemptible cur*: a reply to this epigram was written by Schopenhauer:

> Wundern kann es mich nicht, daß manche die Hunde verleumden,
> Denn es beschämet so oft leider den Menschen der Hund.

> I'm not surpised to hear dogs maligned by their human companions;
> For the example of dogs puts man so often to shame.

5 *niemand mags gern hören*: in the German text, we have substituted the original *Musenalmanach* version (see above, p. viii) of the second line for the metrically impossible traditional reading (*niemand hörts gerne*); both give the same sense.

9 *mentula*: Goethe's speculation that the indecent Latin word for 'penis' was derived from *mens* is interesting but fanciful. His complaint about the word *Schwanz* should apply equally to 'penis', which also means 'tail'.

10 *boys*: this catholicity of sexual taste in the younger Goethe is needless to say not well documented, though it has been suggested (see Boyle, *Goethe*, 303 f.) that his feelings for Charlotte von Stein's young son Fritz, whom she permitted to live in Goethe's house for three years during the period of his infatuation with her, were not always purely paternal or avuncular. The somewhat illogical argument of the epigram seems to be that girls have an advantage over boys in possessing, so to speak, two vaginas, thus reducing, as well as increasing, the statistical risk that the lover will encounter (as in 8) a passage as wide as a Venetian canal. E. M. Wilkinson's illuminating essay ('Sexual Attitudes') insists that this rather cynical *boutade* must be read in the context of Goethe's tender love-play with Christiane-Faustina. It can at any rate stand as a particularly concrete example of the conciliatoriness so much lauded and criticized in the author of *Faust*, that aversion to stark alternatives which pervades all levels of his thought and work.

11 *lacertae*: Goethe uses a Germanized form of the Latin word for lizard (*lacerta*, plural *lacertae*).

12 *spelunca*: the Latin word for 'cave' has acquired in its German form *Spelunke* the meaning of a low or disreputable lodging-house.

20 *Apostle*: referring to his book, Goethe cites the story in Acts 10: 9–16, of the hungry St Peter who dreams that he is offered a mixed bundle, descending from heaven, of ritually 'clean' and 'unclean' meats: they have all been cleansed by God. The allusion would have little point if Goethe's Venetian miscellany were intended to be purged of its indecencies.

21 *Bettina*: Epigrams 21 to 27 are concerned with the small group of street acrobats whose performances Goethe watched in Venice; they seem to have been a family group, their leader being the father of some of the young female performers, including 'Bettina' (see Introduction pp. xxxii f.).

24 *your maiden flower*: Goethe's warning to Bettina that simply by plying her trade she may lose her virginal status can no doubt be read as an early example of the Romantic motif of the dehumanizing effects of art; the same could be said of 25.

26 *Bruegel . . . Dürer*: the appreciation here shown by Goethe for the grotesque and fantastic elements in the work of Pieter Bruegel (*c*.1525–69) and Albrecht Dürer (1471–1528; the allusion here seems to be to his *Apocalypse* woodcuts) is interestingly at variance with his usual classicistic conception of art. As Rasch ('Die Gauklerin Bettine') points out, however, it is equally significant for Goethe that at the end of her performance, which appears to confound the laws of nature, Bettina safely resumes her normal upright posture on the ground, thus so to speak restoring the natural order and resolving the dissonance.

28 *medicine you need*: for the general significance of this epigram see Introduction p. xli.

29 *Christ*: in the published epigram, the last word has always been replaced by a cross or dagger sign (†). In the autograph MS H55 (see Staiger edn., 510 f. and Eibl edn., 1140 f.) there is no doubt that Goethe wrote *Christ* (= *Christus*); he was probably, as Staiger suggests, thinking chiefly of the crucifixes which he saw all over Italy and found particularly distasteful. According, however, to a tradition going back to the poet's son August, his father in this epigram had (or claimed to have) nothing more shocking in mind than a list of four malodorous things, of which the fourth was to be the breaking of wind.

31 *Lais*: the name of a well-known Greek courtesan.

St Paul . . . Stephen: for the new liberating religion which Christ is now called upon to launch, the poet is willing to be his chief apostle (with the full zeal of the sudden convert) or for that matter his first martyr.

32 *Willst du die Freuden*: for this whole epigram we have adopted the metrically and otherwise superior *Musenalmanach* text (see p. viii).

37 *A disc on a string*: the yo-yo, for centuries an intermittently fashionable toy, was well known at the time of the French Revolution; more recently it was a craze in the 1930s.

40 *The Hours*: the *Horae* were the goddesses of the hours and seasons and time in general.

41 *Parted from all my joy*: the earlier *Musenalmanach* text here reads *Freuden*, which we have adopted; in the collected editions this has changed, by revision or oversight, to *Freunden* ('parted from all my friends'); both readings are plausible.

   in this Neptunian city: as a kind of concluding statement, this epigram has from the first printing onwards generally stood at the end of the published Venetian cycle. The total canonical count has been either 103 or 104, depending on editorial policy as to the inclusion of the interpolated encomium on Karl August (see above, note on 1).

THE DIARY

THE DIARY: in both the surviving MSS (see Introduction) the date '1810' immediately follows the word '*Tagebuch*', which may mean that Goethe intended this to be part of the title itself (*The Diary 1810*, or *The 1810 Diary*).

Venus: from Tibullus (1. 5. 39 f.). The Latin distich in fact begins 'Saepe aliam tenui . . .', giving the sense: '(Often) I held another woman in my arms, but as I was about to take my pleasure Venus reminded me of my lady and deserted me.' Goethe omits the first word and disregards the context of the lines, thus adapting them to the situation in his own poem, of which they are an integral and highly important component.

116 *love-knots*: the spells (usually involving the symbolic tying of a knot) by which loving or jealous women were thought to render men impotent with any other partner.

119 *lady (Herrin)*: i.e. his future wife (cf. the 'domina' of the Tibullus epigraph).

135 *Thy . . . Christe*: the German text literally reads 'before thy wretched cross, bloodstained Christ . . .'. Goethe originally seems to have written 'blutströmig', then 'blutstriemig', finally adopting 'blutrünstig'; all

these mean 'running with blood' (from wounds etc.) though 'blutrünstig' in twentieth-century use has come to mean 'bloodthirsty'. Goethe's provocative combination of this line with the next, though thematically central to the whole poem, has always been found particularly offensive, so that in nearly all the earlier printings of *Das Tagebuch* lines 135 f. are editorially reworded or partly excised (cf. Introduction).

136 *Iste*: Goethe's choice of the Latin pronoun 'iste' (= that, this) to denote the penis is discussed in the Introduction. So far as its precise Latin meaning is concerned, 'iste' has been called the 'demonstrative of the second person' because it was chiefly (but by no means exclusively) used to refer to something near or belonging or related to, or otherwise associated with, the person addressed ('that thing of yours', 'that of which you speak', etc.). The second-person element however is often notional or virtually absent, the reference being merely to persons or things of which the hearer is aware ('that . . . which you have heard of', 'the well-known . . .'; cf. in German 'das bewußte . . .'). The 'iste' forms also frequently carried a derogatory or contemptuous nuance: 'isti' 'these persons', 'iste' 'that fellow' (whom we are discussing), 'iste insolens barbarus' ('that insolent savage'). A usage that comes close to Goethe's occurs in the *Priapea* (no. LVI), when the god addresses an intruder to the garden with a threatening reference to his own displayed phallus (cf. Elegy I) which he calls simply 'ista', with the feminine noun 'mentula' (the obscene word for penis) understood, i.e. 'this (prick which you see)'; the same euphemistic use of the first person possessive 'mea' by itself (for 'mea mentula') is also found. Goethe's 'der Iste' is thus (the narrator addressing the reader) 'this thing of mine (which I am telling you about)'; the definite article 'der' is in the context equivalent to 'my', as commonly in German. One might indeed say that all three grammatical persons are here implicitly present: the *I* to whom the recalcitrant organ belongs, the *you* to whom the poet has been describing its behaviour, and the thing *it*self from which he is now so ruefully dissociated. It is not clear whether 'Iste' and (l. 153) 'Meister Iste' in Goethe's sense are entirely his own coinage in German, though this seems probable.

153 *wise Sir Iste*: the word 'Meister' is difficult to translate consistently. In the present context, both it and the English equivalent 'master' denote the master of a trade or skill, a mature practitioner no longer a novice, but the two words diverge in their connotations. 'Meister' is also the honorific title for such a master (as in 'Meister Hans Sachs', 'Meister Ariost', etc.), whereas in English 'Master So-and-so', as a slightly ironic title, suggests a young boy ('Master John', 'Master Smith', or

Dickens's homophonous 'Master Bates'). This English nuance seems
appropriate in lines 87 and 128, and perhaps justifies my insertion of
'young master' into the notorious line 136. In 153, however (the only
occurrence of the complete phrase 'Meister Iste' in the poem), the
sense of the German title 'Meister' is more prominent, and requires
some such paraphrase as I have adopted here.

185 ff. *But . . . owe*: the ironies and ambiguities of the closing stanza are
discussed in the Introduction. For translation purposes I have assumed
the following interpretations: (*a*) 'stolpern' (stumble) refers to the
narrator's near-adultery (paralleling the daemonic temptation of the
first stanza, l. 7), and not, as has sometimes been thought, to his
temporary impotence; (*b*) the statement 'zwei Hebel vermögen viel',
i.e. two forces (literally 'two levers') can do much, means not that the
two forces (duty and love) are in conflict but that they are both our
allies, though one is greater than the other (paralleling 'so waltet
was . . .' in l. 8, i.e., literally, 'something prevails' and 'saves our vir-
tue'); (*c*) 'die Pflicht' (duty) is in this context the narrator's (or our)
'plighted troth', his marital duty to be faithful to his wife and potent
with her; and (*d*) 'die Liebe' is the deep sexual passion which not only
drives him into the arms of a stranger, but is also—and chiefly—
directed towards his wife, as a personal love which binds his potency
to her as if with a 'magic love-knot'. It is thus a greater power than
duty, and transcends morality only to reinforce it in an ironic and
unexpected way.

INDEX TO ROMAN ELEGIES

The renumbering of the Elegies adopted in the present edition is given below, with the traditional numbering of the corresponding poems added in brackets. **I and XXIV were omitted in nearly all previous editions, *III and XVII were included in a few as Ia and XIVa.

INDEX TO VENETIAN EPIGRAMS

The canonical and secreted epigrams in the present selection are identified here by the page-numbers (p. 305 etc.) in Staiger's edition (1949, vol. i), and the former also by his numbering '1–104' (see above, note on no. 41).

THE WORLD'S CLASSICS

A Select List

HANS ANDERSEN: Fairy Tales
Translated by L. W. Kingsland
Introduction by Naomi Lewis
Illustrated by Vilhelm Pedersen and Lorenz Frølich

JANE AUSTEN: Emma
Edited by James Kinsley and David Lodge

Mansfield Park
Edited by James Kinsley and John Lucas

J. M. BARRIE: Peter Pan in Kensington Gardens & Peter and Wendy
Edited by Peter Hollindale

WILLIAM BECKFORD: Vathek
Edited by Roger Lonsdale

CHARLOTTE BRONTË: Jane Eyre
Edited by Margaret Smith

THOMAS CARLYLE: The French Revolution
Edited by K. J. Fielding and David Sorensen

LEWIS CARROLL: Alice's Adventures in Wonderland
and Through the Looking Glass
Edited by Roger Lancelyn Green
Illustrated by John Tenniel

MIGUEL DE CERVANTES: Don Quixote
Translated by Charles Jarvis
Edited by E. C. Riley

GEOFFREY CHAUCER: The Canterbury Tales
Translated by David Wright

ANTON CHEKHOV: The Russian Master and Other Stories
Translated by Ronald Hingley

JOSEPH CONRAD: Victory
Edited by John Batchelor
Introduction by Tony Tanner

DANTE ALIGHIERI: The Divine Comedy
Translated by C. H. Sisson
Edited by David Higgins

VIRGIL: The Aeneid
Translated by C. Day Lewis
Edited by Jasper Griffin

HORACE WALPOLE: The Castle of Otranto
Edited by W. S. Lewis

IZAAK WALTON and CHARLES COTTON:
The Compleat Angler
Edited by John Buxton
Introduction by John Buchan

OSCAR WILDE: Complete Shorter Fiction
Edited by Isobel Murray

The Picture of Dorian Gray
Edited by Isobel Murray

VIRGINIA WOOLF: Orlando
Edited by Rachel Bowlby

ÉMILE ZOLA:
The Attack on the Mill and other stories
Translated by Douglas Parmée

A complete list of Oxford Paperbacks, including The World's Classics, OPUS, Past Masters, Oxford Authors, Oxford Shakespeare, and Oxford Paperback Reference, is available in the UK from the Arts and Reference Publicity Department (BH), Oxford University Press, Walton Street, Oxford OX2 6DP.

In the USA, complete lists are available from the Paperbacks Marketing Manager, Oxford University Press, 200 Madison Avenue, New York, NY 10016.

Oxford Paperbacks are available from all good bookshops. In case of difficulty, customers in the UK can order direct from Oxford University Press Bookshop, Freepost, 116 High Street, Oxford, OX1 4BR, enclosing full payment. Please add 10 per cent of published price for postage and packing.